A PASSIONATE LIFE

This devotional journal belongs to:

_____

Life Verse:

_____

_____

_____

_____

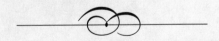

NexGen® is an imprint of
Cook Communications Ministries
Colorado Springs, CO 80918
Cook Communications, Paris, Ontario
Kingsway Communications, Eastbourne, England

A Passionate Life Devotional Journal
© 2005 by Mike Breen and Walt Kallestad

Writers: Liz Lovell, Anne Maclaurin
Cover Design: Brand Navigation, LLC
Cover Photo: PhotoDisc

First Printing, 2005
Printed in Canada
      1 2 3 4 5 6 7 8 9 10 Printing/Year 10 09 08 07 06 05

1-56292-722-1

LIFESHAPES

A

Passionate

LIFE

DEVOTIONAL

JOURNAL

HONOR **HB** BOOKS

Inspiration and Motivation for the Seasons of Life

COOK COMMUNICATIONS MINISTRIES
Colorado Springs, Colorado • Paris, Ontario
KINGSWAY COMMUNICATIONS LTD
Eastbourne, England

INTRODUCTION

Do you long for a passionate relationship with God? Do you long for real community with your friends, family and colleagues? Do you want to change the world around you?

This journal is designed to help you do that as you embark on your own spiritual journey with Jesus as your guide. As you learn more about how to follow Jesus through Scripture verses, devotional prompts, and your personal reflections, we trust you will discover that he is the One who shows you the way, leads you into all truth and gives you the freedom to live a passionate life.

Based on the *LifeShapes* described in the books *A Passionate Life* and *The Passionate Church*, all the shapes used in this journal are about growing and maturing spiritually. How? Just as the first disciples did—by following Jesus, observing him in close relationship with his father, with his followers, and people he met along the way. Those early disciples allowed their relationship with Jesus and with each other to bring about change in their own lives—changes in a motley crew that impacted the world forever.

In each entry, you will discover an aspect of a shape, and you will be given opportunity to reflect, discuss and journal about how God is communicating with you about the principles of that shape in your own life. We've posed some questions, along with space to write a little or a lot as you ponder what God is saying to you.

In addition, you'll see that you've been given extra space in "Going further" and in "And further." From our experience in living out *LifeShapes*, continued application of the shapes will take you deeper in your relationship with God. So the idea behind these extra reflective spaces is for you to use the journal to keep unpacking the principles as God gives you additional insights and to be encouraged as you review how far you've travelled.

Our thanks to Liz Lovell and Anne Maclaurin for their assistance in writing this journal. Their insights and personal reflections drawn from their years of following Jesus and living LifeShapes have deeply enriched the content of these devotionals.

One final word: Journaling is primarily an individual endeavor but the principles of *LifeShapes* are meant to be lived out in community, just as Jesus did life with his first disciples. Why not find a trusted friend who is willing to walk alongside you on this spiritual journey? Give him or her a copy of this journal and then set up times when you can discuss together how God is changing and reshaping your life through the experience and cheer each other on to each new stage in your spiritual life.

Enjoy your journey into a passionate life with Jesus!

How to Use
This Devotional

The devotionals in this journal are all based around the concepts presented in *LifeShapes*. *LifeShapes* takes advantage of our tendency to remember what we see longer than what we hear. Biblical principles connected to basic shapes help you remember how to follow Jesus' example in every aspect of your life. As you read these devotionals, notice that we have connected each to one of the following *LifeShapes*.

The Circle: Jesus marked the beginning of his ministry by calling on all believers to *repent* and *believe* (Mark 1:15). The Circle takes us through the process of repentance and belief and faith so that our lives can be fully changed for Christ.

The Semi-Circle: Every day, week, month, and year of Jesus' ministry was marked by periods of work and rest. He calls upon us to find the same rhythms of fruitfulness and abiding characterized by equal moments of work and rest in our lives (John 15:1-4).

The Triangle: Jesus had the perfect balance in all the relationships of his life—Up with the Father, In with the disciples, and Out with the rest of the world. We can live a balanced and relational life by following the same example of Jesus seen in Matthew 9:35-38.

The Square: Jesus is the greatest leader of all time. And the fact that we all have at least one other person looking to us as an example makes us leaders as well. Use Jesus' example to teach you the four principles of good leadership and personal growth (Mark 1:16-20; Luke 12:32-34; John 15:14-15; Matt. 28:18-20).

The Pentagon: Ephesians 4 tells of the five ministry roles and that we have all been granted at least one. Once you discover the role God designed you for, you can stop striving to be something you aren't meant to be and do something that will truly build up the body of Christ.

The Hexagon: Jesus taught us the perfect prayer in Matthew 6:9-13. Learn the six phrases that Jesus prayed and what he truly meant by them, and your prayer life will become the most effective and dynamic you've ever experienced.

The Heptagon: Biological life has seven basic requirements and our spiritual lives have the same. Practice each of them and your spirit will be renewed and refreshed with the presence of God (1 Pet. 2:4-5).

The Octagon: Evangelism can be a scary thing for those who aren't really sure what they're doing. But Jesus simply tells us to be on the lookout for the *Person of Peace* (Luke 10:5-6). Understanding this concept makes evangelism and discipleship a much simpler task.

For more information on *LifeShapes* and other products available, visit www.LifeShapes.com.

THE TRIANGLE

༄

One of those days Jesus went out to a mountainside to pray,
and spent the night praying to God. When morning came, he called his
disciples to him, and chose twelve of them … He went down with them and stood
on a level place. A large crowd of his disciples was there and a great number
of people … who had come to hear him and to be healed of their diseases.
Those troubled by evil spirits were cured, and the people all tried to touch him,
because power was coming from him and healing them all.
LUKE 6:12-13,17-19

This passage is all about relationships. It's about the relationship Jesus had with his Father, the relationship he had with his community of close friends and the relationship he and his disciples had with other people. This is the Jesus model of relationships.

Describe your relationship with your Father in Heaven, your friends and family, and with other people:

_____

_____

_____

_____

_____

_____

_____

_____

_____

_____

_____

[Jesus said], "I tell you the truth, the Son can do nothing by himself; he can
do only what he sees his Father doing, because whatever the Father does the Son
also does. For the Father loves the Son and shows him all he does."
JOHN 5:19-20

Jesus often withdrew to lonely places—mountain tops, gardens, the side of a lake where it was quiet—to focus on his Father. By recalling the character of the Father, Jesus found purpose and direction. In his Father's presence, Jesus could rest in who he was, where he had come from, and where he was going.

Imagine you are in your favorite place to meet with God. What is he telling you about himself? What is it you want to know from him about who you are and where you are going?

As Jesus and his disciples were on their way, he came to a village where a woman named Martha opened her home to him.
LUKE 10:38

This verse shows the birth of a life-long and vital friendship between Martha, Mary, Lazarus and Jesus. It started so simply but developed so spectacularly because Jesus invested in his relationships with other believers. He also spent a lot of time eating with friends—so much so that his accusers called him a glutton! (Matthew 11:19)

These friends shared their highs and lows with Jesus. They trusted him.
Who are the friends you eat with, laugh with, and trust? How do you think
you could "go deeper" with them?

_____

_____

_____

_____

_____

_____

_____

_____

Jesus came down from the mountain with his disciples and met the crowds
on a level place. This made him accessible to people beyond his inner circle.
He didn't expect people to climb a mountain to meet with him. He had his
group of friends, but that friendship was not exclusive. He and his disciples
extended the sense of community they experienced together to whomever
wanted to join them.

Recall a time when you felt excluded, included. How did each make you
feel? How did each affect your walk with God?

_____

_____

_____

_____

_____

_____

_____

Going further …

And further …

THE TRIANGLE: UP

One of those days Jesus went out to a mountainside to pray,
and spent the night praying to God. When morning came,
he called his disciples to him and chose twelve of them...
LUKE 6:12-13

In the context of the Triangle, Jesus' relationship with his Father represents the dynamic of Up. He is relating to someone who is not constrained by the boundaries of this earth. Jesus' relationship with his Father is not simply about prayer; it's a combination of both being *with* the Father and doing *for* the Father.

In what ways do you have a sense that your relationship with God is limited to times of prayer? How would your life change if you lived as if you were in the presence of God all the time?

"Earlier this year I was chatting to Liz about prayer and saying that it had gone a bit dry. Liz asked, 'Are you doing anything new at the moment?' I said, 'Yes, I have just been given a new workout regime at the gym I go to.' Liz said, 'Why don't you involve Jesus in that new workout?' So, now when I warm up, I use that as a time to give thanks to God. When I move to the resistance work, I chat to Jesus about bringing break-through in other people's lives and my own. Then I move to the 'fit ball' and I work on 'core stability' reminding myself of God's promises to me. When I move to cardio-vascular work, I focus on breathing in the Holy Spirit and keeping my heart healthy. It's much more fun working out with Jesus!"

—Anne

Our natural tendency is to complicate anything related to God. Yes, he deserves our worship but that will flow joyfully out of our more intimate moments with him. Missing those moments? What are the things you enjoy doing? Jesus is there anyway, so why leave him parked on the sidelines? How could you include him in the every day things you enjoy the most? Now consider the less spectacular parts of your life. How might Jesus' presence enliven them?

Read Psalm 104—notice how David simply uses the things he sees around him and prays them back to God.

God delights in revealing himself to his children. Take some time to observe your surroundings. Reflect on what you see and what it reveals to you about him. Use what you see to write a prayer back to God.

Going further …

And further …

THE TRIANGLE: IN

*Then came the day of Unleavened Bread on which the Passover lamb
had to be sacrificed. Jesus sent Peter and John, saying,
"Go and make preparations for us to eat the Passover."*
LUKE 22:7-8

The Passover was one of the most important Jewish festivals. It's significant
that Jesus chose to celebrate this with his close friends. John's version of
events shows the deep nature of their friendship—Jesus washed his disciples'
feet, he called them friends, not servants, he prayed the prayer asking his
Father for oneness for his disciples and those who came after them because
he wanted them to be one in the same way that he and the Father are one.

*"When I was a child we had Jewish neighbors. One year, they invited me
to celebrate the Feast of Tabernacles with them. They had a small shed
built in their garden, which they decorated with vines, grapes and fruit.
It was in this that we had a special meal. This had a profound effect on
me. I'm sure this early childhood experience was the catalyst for my husband, John, and I always including friends in our family celebrations."*

—Liz

What is significant about your family celebrations? What friends could you
include and how might including others change the faith dynamics of these
family times?

_____

_____

_____

_____

_____

Friends, acquaintances, colleagues from work, teammates in sports, fellow members at church—each of us has the potential for community life. Even if your friends live far away, with some effort you can keep in community with them. How intentional are you about gathering those friends and sharing your life with them?

The community of Acts 2:42 is clearly committed to each other in ways that stretch our Western cultural understanding. Yet one of the reasons people were drawn to the early Christians was their evident commitment to one another. What does community look like for you? Why is community so important to your journey of faith?

Another place where we see this commitment to relationship is in the letters of Paul. He visited many developing communities of believers, and his letters show a deep commitment to the group and individuals within each. He even names specific people, people he obviously knew very well, to commend them or to confront them.

It's evident from both of these examples in the New Testament that it is possible to develop deep friendship with people regardless of whether or not you are planted in one geographical area. What kind of investment are you willing to make to establish and develop community within the relationships God has given you?

"When we ignore the call of Jesus to do life together, we suffer."
A PASSIONATE LIFE, CHAPTER 10

Going further ...

_____

_____

_____

_____

_____

_____

_____

_____

_____

_____

And further ...

_____

_____

_____

_____

_____

_____

_____

_____

_____

_____

_____

_____

THE TRIANGLE: OUT

*After this the Lord appointed seventy-two others and sent them two by two
ahead of him to every town and place where he was about to go. He told them,
"The harvest is plentiful, but the workers are few. Ask the Lord of the harvest,
therefore, to send out workers into his harvest field."*
LUKE 10:1-2

The way Jesus lived his life was from a place of engagement with his Father
(Up), relationship with his friends (In), and then together with them into
his society (Out). It can be the same for us—we call this the "flow of grace"
from Up to In to Out. And note that most of the time, Jesus' engagement
with society was in the company of his disciples. Equally, when he sent them
out he asked them to go out in twos—the smallest unit of community in
the kingdom of God.

In what specific ways are you engaging with society as a representative
of the King? Do you have people praying for you? If you plan to show acts
of kindness around your neighborhood, can you do that with your friends?
Jesus taught his disciples to go out and witness from a place of belonging.
Where is your place of belonging and how can you utilize it for outreach?

_____

_____

_____

_____

_____

_____

_____

_____

_____

The practical application of "Out" can look quite different from group to group. Here are some examples:

The worship team of one church signed up in pairs, stationing themselves in the foyer of the church to seek out newcomers. Their assignment was to meet and greet visitors and invite them to join their small group.

Another group put on a Nativity play in a local parking lot. They set up the Nativity and served food and beverages. All of the main characters were played by members of the local community—it's become the main event in their neighborhood at Christmas.

A home group planned a camping trip together. One of the group members had a neighbor who, as a single mom with several children, was struggling. The group decided to invite the family along on their trip, providing them with all the gear and food necessary and including them as part of the community.

How might you show God's love to people around you?

_____

_____

_____

_____

_____

_____

_____

_____

_____

_____

_____

_____

_____

_____

_____

"If we simply stay in our safe zones—our churches, our small groups, our Christian sub-culture—we will not be where the lost are."

A PASSIONATE LIFE, CHAPTER 11

Pray (Up) and talk with the people you have identified as your community (In) about what ideas you have to impact the people to whom Jesus is sending you (Out). What steps can you take to put your plan into action?

Going further …

And further …

THE SEMI-CIRCLE: REST

[Jesus said,] "Take my yoke upon you and learn from me, for I am gentle and humble in heart, and you will find rest for your souls."
MATTHEW 11:29

Imagine you're sitting in a comfortable leather armchair in a home full of beautiful antique furniture. Shafts of sunlight stream through the window. You can hear a grandfather clock ticking and are aware of the steady swing of its pendulum. Allow the regular beat to encourage you into a place of rest. This place of rest is God's plan for you. Take a few minutes to allow the distractions of life to subside as you focus on God's desire for you to receive rest.

How did that go? Did you find yourself distracted by anything—things to do, people to see, jobs left undone, a sense of guilt? What thoughts or concerns were difficult for you to release?

_____

_____

_____

_____

_____

_____

_____

_____

_____

_____

_____

_____

_____

_____

From birth, infants need a regular life pattern that alternates between sleeping and feeding—rest and nutrition are vital for a baby's growth. In fact, the whole of a baby's focus is geared around that fact. As healthy adults, we also need a similar rhythm between rest and work.

Describe the rest/work rhythm of your life. Is there a steady rhythm or is the arc erratic? At which end of the pendulum swing do you spend most of your time? Why?

_____

_____

_____

_____

_____

_____

_____

_____

_____

_____

_____

_____

_____

_____

_____

_____

_____

_____

"As a child growing up in India, I would often visit an Indian family in our local village. When their second baby was born, the mother looped a length of plain sari fabric over the ceiling beams of their simple home. This formed a hammock-like cradle. The newborn baby was placed in this. Friends, visitors, relatives— anyone who passed by would give the hammock a gentle push to cause it to swing. There was a constant gentle motion to and fro as the baby slept."

—Liz

Our lives should be like the rhythmic beat of a clock pendulum or the soothing swing of a hammock in motion as we transition from rest to work. And when we are out of sync, we need people in our lives who will push us gently in the right direction. Who do you know that lives in peace and contentment? What can you learn from the rhythm of his or her life? Explain to God why you think your life is out of snyc and how you plan to get it back on track:

_____

_____

_____

_____

_____

_____

_____

_____

_____

_____

_____

_____

_____

_____

_____

_____

_____

_____

_____

_____

_____

_____

_____

This is what the Sovereign LORD, the Holy One of Israel, says: "In repentance and rest is your salvation, in quietness and trust is your strength."
ISAIAH 30:15

Going further …

_____
_____
_____
_____
_____
_____
_____
_____
_____
_____
_____
_____
_____

My soul finds rest in God alone; my salvation comes from him.
PSALM 62:1

And further …

_____
_____
_____
_____
_____
_____
_____
_____
_____

THE SEMI-CIRCLE:
REST TO WORK

❧

He who dwells in the shelter of the Most High will
rest in the shadow of the Almighty.
PSALM 91:1

L et's ask a question here: What was the first activity humans did on earth? Work or rest? Go on, you've got a fifty percent chance of the right answer—take a guess! The creation narrative in Genesis records that God made the earth in six days, and on the seventh day he rested. Humans were made on the sixth day—so the first thing we did with God after we were created was to rest. From that place of rest we went to work—also with God (Gen. 1:26-27, 2:2).

How is your week organized—do you plan your rest before you plan your work? Do you go on vacation to recover from work or to be refreshed in order to work? How could you redesign your rest periods?

_____

_____

_____

_____

_____

_____

_____

_____

_____

_____

_____

_____

_____

Are there changes you want to make in your patterns of rest and work in your days, weeks, months, years? You can start to implement changes today. Look for a time and place of rest in your normal daily schedule. For example, is your lunch or coffee break taken "on the run" or is it a time of rest, however brief, in your day?

Is the fact that God wants you to rest a turning point in your life? Use the space below to observe and reflect, then discuss your week's schedule with a trusted friend. Next, record here how you plan to be intentional about your rest and who will encourage you to act on your plan:

Work is not a result of man's fall into sin—it is not part of the curse. God gave Adam work to do before sin arrived on the scene (Genesis 2:15). Work in balance with rest is a natural expression of God's creative and productive nature in us. What do you think Adam's workday looked like? Did he get up, spend a bit of time with God and then go reluctantly into the garden to till the land from 9-5 before wearily slinking back to meet up with God again?

Several times in Genesis, God's work of creation is described with the phrase "It was good." We are made in God's image—God wants our work to be good. Maybe it's time to redefine what constitutes a good day! Is your work satisfying to you? To God? Why or why not? Describe a workday that both you and God would say was "good." What part did rest play in making it a good day?

_____

_____

_____

_____

_____

_____

_____

_____

_____

_____

_____

_____

_____

_____

_____

_____

_____

_____

_____

_____

_____

_____

_____

Going further …

And further …

THE SEMI-CIRCLE:
WORK TO REST

❧

And God blessed the seventh day and made it holy, because on it
he rested from all the work of creating that he had done.
GENESIS 2:3

We are establishing the rhythm here: rest to work, and now, work to rest. Rest can have many different components but fundamentally it's a time of refreshment, relaxation, and "*re*-creation." Some people recharge best on their own—reading a book, going for a walk, driving their sports car, working out, playing the piano, painting, writing poetry, etc. Other people "re-create" best in the company of others—playing a round of golf, shopping and coffee with friends, going to a movie or the theater, going out for a meal, or entertaining at home.

How do you "re-create"?

_____

_____

_____

_____

_____

_____

_____

_____

_____

_____

_____

Regular times of rest give us the opportunity to process what's going on in our lives. It may be that unexpected feelings of sadness or disappointment come to our attention during these times.

A time of rest can also be described as a "valley time" or a season in life—a time when we are walking with God in the shade of the evening instead of the heat of the day or a time apart where doubts and fears surface and we hear the promise of Psalm 23: *Though I walk through the valley of the shadow of death, I will fear no evil, for you are with me; your rod and your staff, they comfort me.*

Those times apart with God—that allow him to tend to our fears and remind us of his presence with us—become treasured moments in our day, our week, in every season of our life. Reflect for a few moments then respond: What has God been showing you in your times of rest about your relationships, your work, your purpose and plans?

_____

_____

_____

_____

_____

_____

_____

_____

_____

_____

_____

"Last year, after a very busy season of work, I went on vacation with a group of friends. I arrived at our vacation spot rather tired—yes, my rhythm of life had gotten out of whack. On the first afternoon, I went for a walk and found myself in a beautiful valley with sheep grazing in fields on either side and surrounded by mountains rising up to a grey sky. As I walked along, I met a wandering sheep on the road. As I tried to guide it back through a gate into a place of safety and feeding, I realized how much I was like the sheep. I had been living outside God's place of safety and refreshment. God was going to use this time of rest to lead me back to his provision."

—Anne

The Lord is my shepherd, I shall not be in want.
He makes me lie down in green pastures,
he leads me beside quiet waters, he restores my soul.
He guides me in paths of righteousness for his name's sake.
Even though...

PSALM 23:1-4

Life is not just about the good times. It's about the good; it's about the bad; and it's about everything in between. Times of rest allow God's presence to tend to every aspect of our being—restoring and guiding regardless of our circumstances. Talk with your Shepherd about what this looks like at this point in your life:

_____

_____

_____

_____

_____

_____

_____

_____

_____

_____

_____

_____

_____

_____

_____

_____

Going further …

And further …

THE SEMI-CIRCLE:
REST TO WORK

❧

Whatever you do, work at it will all your heart,
as working for the Lord, not for men.
COLOSSIANS 3:23

If times of rest are like walking in the valley, then work might be described as times of exploring the mountains. Work is not just what you do for a living—it's not just your job or ministry. These are times of activity, adventure and achievement. They are the times in your life that you remember with satisfaction and pleasure. Make a note of times like this in your life:

_____

_____

_____

_____

_____

_____

_____

_____

_____

_____

_____

_____

_____

_____

_____

_____

_____

Work is a good thing, a God-given activity, as long as it comes from a place of rest. God has made us in his image. He is the creator and, therefore, to work is to be like him—to be creators, to produce something, to be fruitful.

Here are some examples of fruitful work from the Bible: Lydia, the dealer in purple cloth; the midwives who saved the Israelite children; Nehemiah, the cup bearer to the King; Joseph, Prime Minister of Egypt; Bezalel and Oholiab, skilled craftsmen who built the tabernacle in the wilderness; Priscilla and Aquila, tentmakers; the wife and husband in Proverbs 31, and we could go on.

What fruitful work is God calling you to do? How can you take joy in it?

There is a God-given desire in all of us for adventure and exploration. Picture a toddler at the park, firmly attached to the limbs of his parent, until his attention is drawn to a ball tossed in his direction. He wanders a short distance away from his parent, his attention totally focused on the object. Suddenly, the child becomes of aware of a need to return to his parent for security before adventuring out again, perhaps a bit further the next time.

This example shows the rhythm of movement, from a place of security and rest out to adventure and exploration and then back again. In many ways, we are all like a toddler exploring his world under the watchful eyes of a loving parent. The movement from rest to work is a time to grow and explore and be fruitful. The movement from work to rest is a time of retreat and pruning.

The danger of satisfying work is that it can become addictive. It's possible for awhile to leap from mountaintop to mountaintop without taking time to retreat to the valley but that kind of lifestyle can't last forever. It's a bit like becoming an adrenaline junkie—going from extreme to extreme until, after awhile, you can't be satisfied any more and you can't go further without being dangerous to yourself and others.

Unceasing work ceases to produce as much fruit and fruitless work is never satisfying. When have you observed these principles in your own life? How can you implement rest time in your life to make your work more fruitful?

_____

_____

_____

_____

_____

_____

_____

_____

_____

_____

_____

_____

_____

The final verse of Psalm 23 demonstrates the balance between going out and coming back:

Surely goodness and love will follow me all the days of my life,
and I will dwell in the house of the LORD forever.

(The sense here is that David is on the move, venturing out, until he returns to his place of safety, the house of the Lord.)

Going further …

_____
_____
_____
_____
_____
_____
_____
_____
_____

And further …

_____
_____
_____
_____
_____
_____
_____
_____
_____
_____
_____

THE SEMI-CIRCLE:
WORK TO REST

❧

*Jesus said, "I am the true vine, and my Father is the gardener. He cuts off
every branch in me that bears no fruit, while every branch that does bear fruit
he prunes so that it will be even more fruitful."*
JOHN 15:1-2

You may be wondering what connection the process of pruning has with
moving from work to rest. It seems ironic that with fruit-bearing trees the
gardener has to prune back even fruitful branches in order to increase fruitfulness. It makes sense to cut off a dead branch, but its difficult to accept the
truth that pruning back a fruitful branch will actually increase fruitfulness.

It's the same for us. When we are at the fullest extent of our work and fruitfulness, we can anticipate the natural swing of the pendulum to bring us back
into a period of rest and pruning. Rest to work—fruitfulness; work to rest—
pruning. Take note of times when you have seen this dynamic at work in your
life:

_____

_____

_____

_____

_____

_____

_____

_____

The pruning of a fruitful branch takes it right back to the stock of the vine,
so the two are almost indistinguishable. As we are pruned, we come back to a
place of abiding in the vine. Abiding feels unproductive because it is—it's a
time of waiting without yielding, enduring without generating—and in our
activity-driven, results-oriented culture, that feels intolerable even for a season.

But that's Jesus' invitation to his disciples in the same passage:

> *"Remain [abide] in me, and I will remain in you.*
> *No branch can bear fruit by itself; it must remain in the vine.*
> *Neither can you bear fruit unless you remain in me."*
> JOHN 15:4

What is your response when you sense that the Gardener is heading towards you with pruning shears in his hands? Do pruning times frustrate you because you feel inactive? How might you change your frame of mind so that you can truly "abide"?

_____

_____

_____

_____

_____

_____

_____

_____

_____

_____

_____

_____

_____

_____

_____

_____

_____

_____

_____

_____

"*The idea of abiding in Jesus is so key to our future growth as a church that we designate a month in the summer as abiding time.*"*We don't run any programs or business meetings during this month. If people want to get together, they are encouraged to keep it informal and focused on fellowship. Everyone is encouraged to take time to read and pray and simply hang out with God in the way best suited to his or her personality. When I joined the church, this was a tremendous shock to the system. Take a time of rest? Shouldn't I be running around doing things for God? No. I learned that if I am to be fruitful in the whole of my life, I need to allow the pruning to take place and to be brought back to a close intimacy with the Vine— that is Jesus.*"

—Anne

Visualize a pendulum that moves back and forth from "abiding rest" to "fruitful work." Reflect on the Bible verses from this section. How can you apply this rhythm to the whole of your life? Work? Play? Family? Church?

Going further …

And further …

THE CIRCLE: EVENT

*And Mary said: "My soul glorifies the Lord and my spirit rejoices
in God my Savior, ... for the Mighty One has done great
things for me—holy is his name."*
LUKE 1:46,49

On every journey, things happen. In the course of a road trip, you might come around a corner and suddenly have your breath taken away by a stunning view. Or you might just as suddenly hit a rock that punctures your tire, sending you into a ditch. You might discover a great new place to eat, make a new friend or reconnect with an old one. For every event you encounter, you will have a response. How you respond is key.

Life is a journey full of a wide range of events. Spend a few moments thinking about positive events, things which have provoked a change—an unexpected gift, a new job, new home, an inspirational speaker, the birth of a child, a good film, a piece of music. Write these moments down and list the changes they brought about in your life:

_____

_____

_____

_____

_____

_____

_____

_____

_____

_____

_____

Not all life events are positive. In fact, a negative event—loss of a job, an accident or illness, the death of a friend or loved one—can often have more of an impact on us than the positive ones. List the negative events that have most impacted you and describe how they changed your life:

_____

_____

_____

_____

_____

_____

_____

_____

_____

_____

_____

_____

_____

_____

_____

_____

_____

_____

_____

Travelling in the car provides a good example of a certain kind of time— it takes 45 minutes for a school run, an hour and a half into work, eight hours to reach your favorite vacation spot. This type of time in the Bible is described as *chronos* time—linear, regular, clock or calendar time.

What if, during the school run, in one moment of the 45 minutes required, a child runs out in front of the car. This significant point in time is described as *kairos*—an event, an incident, a moment that has the potential to redirect the course of your life.

Life itself is a journey governed by time—the passage of time being *chronos* and the events of life *kairos*. The events you just recorded are *kairos*. Jesus said in Mark 1:15, "The time has come. The kingdom of God is near." The time he talked about was *kairos*. The events of your life are evidence of God's kingdom being near to you. As you learn to trust God with the *kairos* events—whether good or bad—they can become opportunities for growth. God promises that he works all things (*kairos*) for the good of those who love him and he invites you to take part in the process.

Review the lists of *kairos* moments from the previous pages. If you could go back and change your responses to any of the events, which responses would you change? What would you do differently and how might a different response have changed the effect of the event on your life?

_____

_____

_____

_____

_____

_____

_____

_____

_____

_____

_____

_____

_____

_____

_____

_____

_____

_____

"Jesus loves you too much to leave you as you are. As his disciple, you are called to a life of constant renewal, revival—of change. You can find hope and healing for your past, present, and future."

A PASSIONATE LIFE, CHAPTER 3

Going further ...

_____

_____

_____

_____

_____

_____

_____

_____

_____

_____

And further ...

_____

_____

_____

_____

_____

_____

THE CIRCLE: OBSERVE

⌘

*[Jesus said,] "Do not worry about your life ... Look at the birds of the air;
they do not sow or reap or store away in barns, and yet your heavenly Father
feeds them. Are you not much more valuable than they?"*
MATTHEW 6:25-26

For a *kairos* event to cause change in your life, two things need to happen—
you need to recognize that the event is a *kairos* moment and you must
process the event using the principles of the Circle.

Think back to one of the events you recorded in the previous section.
The first part of the process is to "observe." As you journal, ask yourself,
"What actually happened?" and "How did I react?"

Don't try to interpret anything. At this stage, simply record:

_____

_____

_____

_____

_____

_____

_____

_____

_____

_____

_____

_____

_____

Jesus taught his disciples to develop the skill of observation. When they started to worry about their lives, he told them to observe God at work in the world around them (Matt. 6:26). Note that Jesus doesn't rehash the problem, anaylze the disciples or come up with solutions to their worries. Instead, he gets them to observe what is going on around them so that their faith might be released.

Describe your ability to observe things around you. Is observation easy or difficult for you? Why? Name someone in your life who can help you improve your observation skills, like Jesus did for his disciples. List specific ways you'd like them to help you:

_____

_____

_____

_____

_____

_____

_____

_____

_____

_____

_____

_____

_____

_____

_____

"Anne and I visited the Sistine Chapel in Rome at the New Year. I've seen many pictures and books about this work; I had even visited the Sistine previously. Still, this time was very different for me and the impact on my life was much greater. The reason? Anne is an Art History major. She helped me to observe aspects of the ceiling I had never noticed before—like the way Michelangelo painted the dynamic movement of the Father, almost invading our space, in the scenes of creation. This heavenly invasion of my space caused me to worship amidst the hubbub of the holiday crowds."

—Liz

Revisit the event you wrote about on the previous page. Is there anything else you can add to your observation of this event? If you have written mostly facts, consider adding more descriptive words to show how the event made you feel:

_____

_____

_____

_____

_____

_____

_____

_____

_____

Jesus also taught his disciples to observe the physical and use that to inform the spiritual:

> *"Do you not say, 'Four months more and then the harvest.' I tell you, open your eyes and look at the fields! They are ripe for harvest."*
> JOHN 4:35

He was training them to realize that in their culture they knew the season for reaping the harvest. He was also telling them to be aware of the season for spiritual harvesting—in this case, the time was NOW! They went to the Samaritan village where many people came to faith (John 4:39).

Do you take time to observe physical events in light of their spiritual applications? How is your spiritual observation?

_____

_____

_____

Going further …

And further …

THE CIRCLE: REFLECT

[Jesus said,] *"Look at the birds of the air; they do not sow or reap or store away in barns, and yet your heavenly Father feeds them. Are you not much more valuable than they? Who of you can add a single hour to his life? And why do you worry about clothes? See how the lilies of the field grow. They do not labor or spin."*
MATTHEW 6:26-27

The next part of the process is to reflect on what you've just observed. Reflection is active. It's about digging deep to find the reasons for a reaction to an event. Reflection in the Circle is not the same technique of "looking back" used in therapy. It's not like using a mirror to simply see what is there. It's looking beyond the face value—peeling away the layers— to get to the core.

In relation to your "event," keep asking yourself the question "why?" Why did you react in such a way? Reread your answer. Now ask "why?" again. Keep going until you get to the heart of the matter.

_____

_____

_____

_____

_____

_____

_____

_____

_____

_____

_____

Jesus takes his disciples from observation to reflection. After telling them to look at the birds in the air and the flowers in the field, he asks them to dig deeper; "Are you not much more valuable than they?" and "Why do you worry about clothes?"

The reflection for the disciples, which is not recorded in the Bible, may have gone something like this:

"Well, yes, of course we are more valuable than birds—they are a dime-a-dozen. And look at the beautiful detail in those flowers. God did that for something that will wither away tomorrow. So, if the Father looks after them, how much more will he look after us? Get it, Peter?"

What has been the result of worry in your life? Do you think God highly values you? Why or why not? How does your answer affect your relationship with him?

Jesus said, "If you hold to my teaching, you are really my disciples.
Then you will know the truth, and the truth will set you free."
JOHN 8:31-32

Getting to the core of your *kairos* event will help you see the truth God
wants to teach you. In God's truth, there is freedom. What truths do you
think God is showing you through your reflections on your *kairos*? How
do you see those truths setting you free?

Going further ...

And further ...

THE CIRCLE: DISCUSS

❧

Let the word of Christ dwell in you richly
as you teach and admonish one another with all wisdom.
COLOSSIANS 3:16

While the first two parts of the Circle (observe and reflect) may be done alone, the third part (discuss) definitely requires another person to be involved in the process. This is about involving other people in the events of our lives. Jesus never intended for us to live out our Christian lives as "Lone Rangers." On the contrary, he placed us in a body and prayed for our unity—we are part of a community of disciples.

You need to bring to the discussion an account of the event, your observation, and subsequent reflection. It's important that the other person also has time to make observation and reflection as part of the discussion process. This is likely to bring fresh insights so you must be prepared to listen and to engage with one another. How will you choose who you will discuss your *kairos* event with? In a nutshell, describe your observations and reflections:

_____

_____

_____

_____

_____

_____

_____

_____

_____

_____

_____

_____

Remember that "discuss" is part of the Repent half of the Circle—it is the point where you allow someone else to enter into the process, a process you are hoping will result in a different way of thinking that leads to a change in your behavior.

Both parties in a discussion have a role to play—you are either talking or listening but you can't do both at the same time! Think about an experience you have had discussing something important with someone. Do any of these words fit your experience: encouraging, respectful, risky, wise, meaningful, loving, safe, mutual, honest, insightful? After you have discussed your *kairos* event with someone, come back to this page and write about it:

"My daughter Suzie was planning a three-month visit to New Zealand after finishing high school. As a mother, I was naturally concerned about various details of the trip and her safety. I discussed this with Anne. She reminded me about the many young adults I've mentored. Part of their lifestyle is to travel and explore new countries. She encouraged me to respond as a mother releasing her child from one stage of life (teenager) into the next (young adult). It was also a release for me from one stage of motherhood into the next."

—Liz

Parents or authority figures are often the best people to turn to for the steps of the Circle. Take time to read the story of Moses and his father-in-law Jethro in Exodus 18. The "event" was Moses' judging the people in verse 13. It led into the process we've been describing. Can you spot the "observe," "reflect," and "discuss" in verses 14–20?

What are the dynamics of their discussion? How could you mirror the honor and respect Moses showed his father-in-law? How might you share non-confrontational wisdom with others as you observe their "events"?

_____

_____

_____

_____

_____

_____

_____

_____

_____

_____

_____

_____

_____

_____

_____

Going further …

And further …

THE CIRCLE: PLAN

"For I know the plans I have for you," declares the Lord,
"plans to prosper you and not to harm you,
plans to give you hope and a future."
JEREMIAH 29:11

Plan, the next stage in the Circle, provides a forward momentum to your discussion. Discussions can often go round and round without getting anywhere, but intentionally working towards a plan should prevent this from happening. There's no point in engaging in a discussion unless your objective is to come out of it with a plan to help you move forward.

Proverbs 20:18 says to "Make plans by seeking advice." Involve the person or people with whom you discussed your *kairos*. It's good to do this in community and not in isolation because the development and successful completion of a plan is more likely with the contribution and support of different personalities.

For example, a personality which tends to be driven will come up with a highly detailed plan with measurable targets and a deadline; this may not allow space for the Holy Spirit to work. On the other hand, a big picture person who is innovative and creative may struggle with the details and have difficulty in coming up with a workable plan. Working together, there is the opportunity to come up with a "disciplined" plan. Describe your own personality type:

_____

_____

_____

Discipline is not a particularly popular word, but the benefit of having a disciplined life is explained by Solomon at the beginning of Proverbs.

The proverbs of Solomon son of David, King of Israel: for attaining wisdom and discipline; for understanding words of insight; for acquiring a disciplined and prudent life, doing what is right and just and fair.
PROVERBS 1:1-3

How do you react to the idea of a disciplined life? According to your personality, what does a disciplined life look like for you?

_____

_____

_____

_____

_____

_____

_____

_____

_____

_____

_____

_____

_____

"On several occasions, I have worked with young adults as they've planned their weddings. Since so many of them are creative, they come up with all sorts of wonderful ideas, most of which are completely impractical and will not be understood by their parents! In most instances I have encouraged them to go away and write down a short list of things that are really important to their wedding day. I know that what I bring to the planning is an essential reality check, bringing simplicity to their creativity."
—Liz

The point of planning is to bring God's grace into the day-to-day reality of our lives.

"For I know the plans I have for you," declares the LORD, "plans to prosper you and not to harm you, plans to give you hope and a future. Then you will call upon me and come and pray to me, and I will listen to you. You will seek me and find me when you seek me with all your heart."
JEREMIAH 29:11-13

What can you learn from these verses about the process of discovering God's plan for you? How might a faithful understanding of God's plan for you affect the disciplined plans you choose to make for yourself?

_____

_____

_____

_____

_____

_____

_____

_____

_____

_____

_____

_____

_____

_____

"The rule of God in our lives becomes our vision as we let go
of a worry-filled life ... God will take care of all things.
This is the foundation of our planning."
A PASSIONATE LIFE, CHAPTER 5

Going further ...

And further ...

THE CIRCLE: ACCOUNT

"This is the verdict: Light has come into the world, but men loved darkness instead of light because their deeds were evil ... But whoever lives by the truth comes into the light, so that it may be seen plainly that what he has done has been done through God."
JOHN 3:19,21

Account is the key opportunity for the plans you have made to come to fruition! It's the natural next step after your discussion and planning time with your trusted friend. To account is to agree that you will act, usually within an agreed time frame. Accountability takes place between two or three trusted friends of the same gender. The accountability is mutual in that each person has permission to speak into the other person's life, in this instance using the Circle. (But all the other shapes can also be used in the account ability process.)

Accountability may include times of encouragement and challenge—even confrontation! This is all in the process of keeping our lives and actions open and honest—"in the light" and not hidden away. An accountability partner is less of a policeman and more of a coach cheering you on to your goal. How does this model of accountability agree or disagree with your present experience with accountability?

_____

_____

_____

_____

_____

Therefore confess your sins to each other and pray for each other
so that you may be healed.
JAMES 5:16

"You may have noticed the number of times Liz and I mention talking
things through with each other. Is this because Liz is a good cook and
I am always at her house eating meals and chatting? No. The main reason
is that we are in an accountability friendship, as is every member of the
church we attend."

—Anne

"For me it is about knowing that Anne wants the best for me and there
isn't any judgment going on."

—Liz

Though it may seem counter-intuitive, accountability is about freedom.
It is in the context of "mutual" and "trusted" that you can bring things into
the light. Are you open to not having anything in your life which hasn't
been shared with at least one other person? Why or why not?

_____

_____

_____

_____

_____

_____

_____

_____

_____

_____

_____

_____

_____

An important part of the challenge is that you give permission to your accountability partner to spot where you are holding unforgiveness against another person. The application of Matthew 18:15 stops a seed of hurt from becoming a bitter and destructive root in your life:

[Jesus said,] *"If your brother sins against you, go and show him his fault, just between the two of you. If he listens to you, you have won your brother over."*

Why is it so much easier to blame someone else instead of taking responsibility? What part do fear and pride play in your reluctance to be authentic with others?

_____

_____

_____

_____

_____

_____

_____

_____

What do you see as the long-term consequences in your own life of not developing accountable relationships?

_____

_____

_____

_____

_____

_____

Going further …

And further …

THE CIRCLE: ACT

T his is the final part of the process. You've observed, reflected, discussed, planned, accounted and NOW it's time to act! It may be that the action is to forgive another person or to buy a car or to engage in a fitness regime or to "actively" do nothing. Sometimes the most difficult action is to not do anything in response to the event.

> *"I remember an occasion where my sister and I had a bit of a tiff. I came home rather ruffled and my plan was to call her and argue more for my point of view. Before I did this I was accountable to Liz who said, 'Why do you need to do that? What's the point? You actually understand the reasons why she was angry with you, so simply forgive her and don't try to make any more out of it.'"*

—Anne

Have you ever advised someone else about an action they were about to take? How did that go?

_____

_____

_____

Think back to some of the ways you've acted in past situations. Write your actions and next to them comment on what you now think of the action you took:

_____

_____

_____

_____

_____

_____

_____

How do you think you would have acted in these situations if you'd had the benefit of the Circle?

_____

_____

_____

_____

_____

_____

_____

_____

_____

_____

_____

Convictions and intentions that are kept inside and not acted on have little to do with faith. Faith is active. In the story of the wise and foolish builders, Jesus taught that it was vital to put what we've heard into practice.

> *Therefore everyone who hears these words of mine and puts them*
> *into practice is like a wise man who built his house on the rock.*
> MATTHEW 7:24

"My boss and I had worked out a plan of action, using the Circle to solve a difficult situation. We both knew it would be quite testing for me, and, as I left the room, he said to me, 'Now when you go back to your office, don't sit and delay and think about this. Go back and just do it.' When I got back I did not delay. I took his direction and made the phone calls I had to make. Taking immediate accountable action brought about a profound sense of achievement and relief."

—Anne

Let's take another look at Moses and Jethro. You've already identified the "observe," "reflect," and "discuss" steps of the Circle in Exodus 18:13–20. Now see if you can find "plan," "account," and "act" in verses 21–26.

The result of this event and process was that it brought relief and release to Moses, making him a more effective leader and preserving his relationships. In fact, it brought about change for a whole nation of people and it meant that Moses as their leader could do what God had called him to do instead of the day-to-day details that were overwhelming him.

Jethro was able to release Moses, and Moses released Jethro—Moses sent him on his way (vs. 27). Jethro had completed what God had called him to do and it was time to move on. The Circle leads us to move on from events; it stops us from getting stuck in one place.

Are you resting on the laurels of past accomplishments? Is there an area of your life where you sense you may be stuck? What needs to happen so that you are released to respond to God's prompting to move on?

Going further …

And further …

THE CIRCLE: PROCESS

❦

[Jesus said,] "The time has come ... The kingdom of God is near. [event]
Repent and believe the good news!" [process]
MARK 1:15

We started the Circle by describing an event and then took you through a six-stage process. In this final section of the Circle, we want to help you summarize the process.

The first half of the Circle—observe, reflect and discuss—is the part where we repent. The original meaning of the Greek word for repent, *metanoia,* means a "change of mind or heart." It's a change to our inner working brought about by external events and processed in community.

What immediately springs to mind when you hear the word "repent"? How does the idea of it being a "change of mind" bring a sense of freedom to you?

_____

_____

_____

_____

_____

_____

_____

_____

_____

_____

_____

_____

_____

_____

The second half of the Circle requires us to believe, and the evidence of that belief is putting our plans into accountable action. Often faith and belief are viewed as concepts, but as you can see with the Circle, there is always practical action involved. This is the exercise of faith.

What are some practical steps that your faith might be calling you to take? How might you ask those in your community to hold you accountable to these steps?

"There is a real sense of empowerment and freedom for me to know that repentance is not about feeling sorry for myself but allowing God to change the inner workings of my life. The Circle has allowed me to process the events of my life in a much shorter time. I can move on and into the future more quickly and with greater excitement. I now look forward to the action."

—Liz

It's essential to know that as you complete one Circle, it usually leads to another, like the interconnected loops of a Slinky. Our life is a series of inter-locking Circles leading us forward from one event to another. That's why we have the "Going futher" sections at the end of each devotional. It's likely that the action you take will lead to a further event.

The exciting reality is that the kingdom of heaven comes nearer in our lives every time we take action as a result of an event. The size of the specific event is immaterial—it can be as mundane as planning what movie to see or as significant as deciding to change jobs. It's truly good news—the kingdom of God is near!

How have the principles of the Circle empowered you to live a more passionate life?

Going further …

And further …

THE SQUARE: DISCIPLESHIP 1

❦

[Jesus said,] *"I am the good shepherd; I know my sheep and my sheep know me—just as the Father knows me and I know the Father."*
JOHN 10:14-15

As followers of Jesus, we are all sheep who are getting to know his voice and learning to follow him. The Square describes four stages of our development as disciples—learners and leaders of other learners who desire to live passionately. At the first stage, known as D1 for short, we answer the call to some new challenge or adventure.

Can you recall a time when you started something new? How about your first job, moving into a new home, starting a relationship, your first attempt at driving a car? Describe your main reactions and emotions to these things. How do you handle new things in your life today?

_____

_____

_____

_____

_____

_____

_____

_____

_____

_____

_____

_____

_____

"I remember clearly driving to my first day at work. I had graduated from college with a degree in Art History and Psychology and felt ready to start earning some money. It was a day of excitement, anticipation, and enthusiasm. When I got there, I found out how little I actually knew. Studying Leonardo da Vinci for four years does not exactly equip you for handling customer complaints!"

—Anne

Excitement, anticipation, enthusiasm, low experience—this describes the experience of being in D1. Think about the disciples for a moment.

"Come, follow me," Jesus said, "and I will make you fishers of men."
At once they left their nets and followed him.
MARK 1:17-18

At this point, do you think the disciples understood what being "fishers of men" meant? How much experience do you think they had for the new task they were taking on? They enthusiastically answered Jesus' invitation to follow him but they did not have a clue what they were getting themselves into. Jesus simply directed them to follow him—they had no more detail than that.

This stage of learning is important for your faith to advance. Sometimes you just have to "go for it" without really understanding where you will end up. Why do you think the disciples were ready to leave everything to follow Jesus?

_____

_____

_____

_____

_____

_____

_____

_____

_____

_____

This is the moment where Jesus, in effect, said to his disciples, "I'm bringing in a new way of living—this is your opportunity to watch and learn."

Think of a specific situation where you see Jesus working in your life. How can you make the most of the opportunity to watch Jesus working? What do you think you might learn from watching Jesus at work?

_____

_____

_____

_____

_____

_____

_____

_____

_____

_____

_____

_____

_____

_____

_____

_____

_____

_____

"When we start out on a new trail, we need a strong,
confident leader to show us the way."
A PASSIONATE LIFE, CHAPTER 13

Going further …

And further …

We all know the feeling when the initial excitement wears off and we wonder, "What have I gotten myself into?!" Our confidence takes a nose dive as we recognize just how inexperienced and ill-equipped we really are for the situation we are in and we can't seem to conjure up the vision that put us there. This is when we start to second-guess ourselves and worry seems to take over.

The disciples started to worry when they realized that the Pharisees and other religious leaders were turning against Jesus—and far from making peace with them, Jesus was confronting them. Where was that going to leave the disciples?

Perhaps you have started something recently where the initial excitement has worn off. Are you thinking, "What's the point?" Talk to Jesus about that here:

Jesus counseled his disciples by saying,

*"Therefore I tell you, do not worry about your life, what you will eat or drink;
or about your body, what you will wear ... Who of you by worrying can add
a single hour to his life? ... But seek first his kingdom and his righteousness,
and all these things will be given to you as well."*
MATTHEW 6:25,27,33

What was Jesus doing here? Jesus was spending time with the disciples,
not judging them for worrying, but coaching them through the difficult time.
He reminded them of God's promise to give them security. He then reminds
them of the vision—the vision that gives their lives significance.

Discouragement is inevitable but if you can persevere, God promises to
help you during the struggle and meet you with joy on the other side of
despair. When you feel as if you're failing, you can turn to Jesus for words
of encouragement. As you spend time with him in the Word and in prayer,
he can coach you back into a place of excitement and passion.

What specific situations require a strengthening of your heart right now?
Can you give them to the Lord? If you feel a lack of excitement and drive,
where can you turn to hear the reaffirming truth of Christ?

Without a vision, the people perish.
PROVERBS 29:18

Security and significance are best understood under the umbrella of God's provision and kingdom. When we're in D2, we need to be reminded of God's care for us and his plan for our lives. We need to be reminded of his vision for God's kingdom in this place and at this time so that the wonder of who he is and what he is doing recaptures our hearts. We need a fresh experience with God's grace.

What is God's vision for you at this time and place in your life? Are there specific areas where you feel you are perishing? How can you allow Jesus to re-envision you?

_____

_____

_____

_____

_____

_____

_____

_____

_____

_____

_____

_____

_____

_____

_____

Going further ...

And further ...

&

While D2 is the most painful part of developing as a disciple, it is also the time when you find out who your real friends are. As Jesus spent time with the disciples during their "down" times, he proved that he understood them and cared for them. As they moved to the next stage (D3), they found out that he also trusted them.

Take some time to read John 13–17 and reflect on the amazing transformation occuring in the relationship between Jesus and his close group of disciples. They had been through the hard times together and come through to a place of mutual friendship and accountability.

> *"I remember a time when I became ill and incredibly tired. As I told people what I was going through, I discovered who my true friends were. Some friends couldn't cope with me being tired all the time and backed off, others came and made sure that practical things were done—they stocked my fridge with food and cooked my meals. They were simply there for me."*
>
> —Anne

If D2 is a time to share the difficulties of life with Jesus and with your community of friends, then D3 brings both a bolder reality and a new depth to those relationships.

How open are you about the difficulties in your life? Have you lost friends? Who are some of the people you've found who stood through the test? What is your relationship like with those friends?

_____

_____

_____

_____

_____

_____

_____

_____

Going around the Square from D2 to D3 is a process and no one can tell you exactly when you will make the transition from one stage to the next. At some point, however, hanging out with Jesus and friends and allowing them to re-envision you leads naturally to the place of mutual friendship and trust.

Jesus sat down opposite the place where the offerings were put and watched the crowd putting their money into the temple treasury. Many rich people threw in large amounts. But a poor widow came and put in two very small copper coins, worth only a fraction of a penny. Calling his disciples to him, Jesus said, "I tell you the truth, this poor widow has put more into the treasury than all the others. They all gave out of their wealth; but she, out her poverty, put in everything—all she had to live on."
MARK 12:41-43

It is obvious from Scripture that Jesus and his disciples spent time together. In the beginning, the disciples watched and listened while Jesus taught. On this occasion, Jesus included his disciples in the observations and reflections he made about the widow's offering. Jesus' growing relationship with the disciples was intentional—it didn't just happen.

Are you intentional about building deeper friendships? Why or why not? How do you and your group of friends invest time in each other?

"You are my friends if you do what I command. I no longer call you servants, because a servant does not know his master's business. Instead, I have called you friends, for everything that I learned from my Father I have made known to you."
JOHN 15:14-15

Jesus desires for us to enter into a deeper relationship with him—a more mutual one—yet often we willingly settle for a lesser relationship, a servant/master relationship. We serve out of obligation and obey out of fear of punishment. And, in the process, we miss out on his invitation to join him on a passionate adventure.

Reflect on the difference between a servant of God and a friend of God. What does it mean to be a friend of God? Which of Jesus' commands is pulling on your heart and how can you respond to it so that you may enter into a deeper relationship with him?

_____

_____

_____

_____

_____

_____

_____

_____

_____

_____

_____

_____

_____

_____

_____

_____

Going further …

And further …

❦

[Jesus said,] *"In a little while you will see me no more,*
and then after a little while you will see me."
JOHN 16:16

The disciples had become close companions to Jesus, sharing meals with him, hearing the nature of his love for them expressed through his love for the Father. They had made the transition from servants to friends. It was at this point that Jesus told them that he would be leaving them.

The disciples were understandably confused by this revelation—saying goodbye to someone you love and trust is never easy. After all they had been through together, how could their leader abandon them? It is at this point that Jesus reveals that God's way is always best:

"But I tell you the truth: It is for your good that I am going away.
Unless I go away, the Counselor will not come to you;
But if I go, I will send him to you."
JOHN 16:7

When you've been involved in something really good, it's difficult to comprehend that something better may be just around the corner. Think back to times when this has happened in your life. how have you seen the promise fulfilled?

_____

_____

_____

_____

_____

_____

_____

_____

Jesus had led his disciples to the point where they were ready to take on the mission that he had started. It was time for them to own the task of making disciples themselves:

"Therefore go and make disciples of all nations, baptizing them in the name of the Father and of the Son and of the Holy Spirit."
MATTHEW 28:19

We can see through the Acts of the Apostles that the disciples did just that. As they took up the Great Commission, they brought other people around the Square, as Jesus had with them, before releasing them for ministry, too. Making disciples who make disciples is what it is all about!

The fact that you're a follower of Jesus can be credited to generation after generation of disciples living through the Square. Are you ready to follow in their footsteps—to fill the fishermen's shoes? Where might you start?

The principles of the Square can be applied to many areas of life—in business, in parenting, in ministry—wherever you are called upon to be a leader. A good leader takes on that responsibility with the full understanding that success will mean letting go. The whole point of the Square is to get someone to the point where he or she can do the job without you.

Think about specific people in your family, your church, your workplace or your community. Who are you leading around the Square at the moment? How can you identify which stage of the Square they are in and use the leadership principles of Jesus to move them forward? Is it time to let go?

Going further …

And further …

THE PENTAGON:
INTRODUCTION

❧

Each one should use whatever gift he has received to serve others,
faithfully, administering God's grace in its various forms.
1 PETER 4:10

The first four shapes apply to any character type or personality—they are ways of living. But the Pentagon gives an opportunity to find out what our role is in the community of faith. It allows us to understand our place and purpose in the body of Christ and where we will be most effective.

Take time to describe your personality. Who are you? Who has God made you to be?

_____

_____

_____

_____

_____

_____

_____

_____

_____

_____

_____

_____

_____

_____

_____

_____

But to each one of us grace has been given as Christ apportioned it ...
It was he who gave some to be apostles, some to be prophets,
some to be evangelists, and some to be pastors and teachers.
EPHESIANS 4:7,11

Apostle, prophet, evangelist, pastor, teacher—as you learn more about each role, you will be able to see which one of these five is your natural role. It will also enable you to identify times in your life when God may be calling you to develop one of the other ministries in order to accomplish the work he has given you to do.

"My natural base is a teacher—I've even been employed as one. In the context of parenting, that's the natural expression of how I relate to my children. However, there are many occasions when I need to relate to them using the other ministries. There are times I need to be a pastor, bringing comfort and security. At other times I will act as a prophet, speaking God's revelation into their lives. I'm learning to develop as an apostle as I lead them into new things. As an evangelist, I aim to operate an open home where it's easy for Suzie and Sam to bring their friends."

—Liz

What is your "gut reaction" about which ministry role applies to you? Why?

_____

_____

_____

_____

_____

_____

_____

_____

In his letter to the believers in Ephesus, Paul highlights the five key roles that are essential to the effective life of the church. The purpose of Jesus giving us these roles is to equip us for acts of service which build up the body until we are united and mature in faith and so receive the fullness of Christ in our lives.

> *... to prepare God's people for works of service, so that the body of Christ*
> *may be built up until we all reach unity in the faith and in the*
> *knowledge of the Son of God and become mature,*
> *attaining to the whole measure of the fullness of Christ.*
> EPHESIANS 4:12-13

What do you think the fullness of Christ looks like in your life? In your church and community?

Going further …

And further . …

THE PENTAGON: APOSTLE

❧

What is an apostle? Apostles are people who love the new thing—
they see existing opportunities and seek out new ones. They are
entrepreneurial. They are great at networking with people and inspiring
others with their vision. They naturally gather and lead people—even if
that's not their particular job at the time!

They enjoy dreaming dreams and making them happen, strategizing.

An apostle often imagines, initiates, excites, envisions, and can be described
as courageous and confident. Describe a time or two in your life when you
have functioned as an apostle:

_____

_____

_____

_____

_____

_____

_____

_____

_____

_____

_____

_____

_____

_____

_____

_____

_____

_____

_____

Some examples from the Bible:

Jesus—the sent one from God (John 3:16, Heb 3:1)
David—shepherd and king of Israel (Ezek. 34, 37)
Joseph—precocious teenager and Egypt's prime minister (Gen. 37, 41)
Shiphrah and Puah—Hebrew midwives in Egypt (Exod. 1)
Lydia—business woman and church founder in Philippi (Acts 16)
Paul—persecutor turned apostle (Acts 9:1-31)

Business-minded people, entrepreneurs, explorers, leaders—what are some characteristics these men and women have in common? Can you recognize apostles among the people you know and in your community of faith?

This may not be your natural role, but now that you've reflected on biblical and personal examples, can you think of times in your life when you've had to act in this way? How might you use this ministry gift in the future?

_____

_____

_____

_____

_____

_____

_____

_____

_____

_____

_____

_____

_____

_____

_____

_____

_____

_____

_____

_____

_____

_____

_____

_____

"God has high goals for the church, and he works out these goals
in the daily lives of believers."
A PASSIONATE LIFE, CHAPTER 15

Going further …

And further …

THE PENTAGON: PROPHET

W hat is a prophet? Prophets are people who are aware of the times in which they live and listen to God for those times. They stand as bridges where heaven and earth touch. They encourage others to hear what God is saying. They use their gifts to build up other people. They act on inspiration; they are creative and often misunderstood.

They enjoy being alone with God, waiting, listening. They have a passion for prayer, intercession, and worship.

Prophets are often identified by their propensity for waiting, resting, reflecting, and seeking God's heart. Describe times in your life when you have exhibited the characteristics of a prophet:

Some examples from the Bible:

Jesus—prophetic in what he says and does;
He also prophesies his own future (Matt. 17:12).
Noah—his obedience to God's word saved humanity (Gen. 6-9)
Elijah—listened to God speak and was obedient (1 Kings 17-19)
Anna and Simeon—waiters and watchers for the revelation (Luke 2)
Deborah—wife, prophetess, and leader of Israel (Judg. 4:4)
John the Baptist—pointed others to "The Way" (Matt. 3)

Visionaries, artists, poets, musicians, writers, and composers—what characteristics do these men and women share? Can you recognize prophets among the people you know?

_____

_____

_____

_____

_____

_____

_____

_____

_____

_____

_____

_____

_____

_____

_____

_____

_____

_____

This may not be your natural role, but now that you've reflected on biblical examples, can you think of times in your life when you've had to act in this way? How might you use this ministry gift in the future?

_____

_____

_____

_____

_____

_____

_____

_____

_____

_____

_____

_____

_____

The term "prophet" makes some in the church nervous because they equate it with telling the future. On the contrary, someone in this role demonstrates more than ordinary spiritual and moral insight. He or she has learned to read the culture, read the Bible, listen to God's voice and speak God's truth.

Do you agree that each and every ministry role listed in Ephesians 4 has a place in the church today? Why or why not?

_____

_____

_____

_____

Going further …

And further …

THE PENTAGON: EVANGELIST

What is an evangelist? Evangelists are people who are passionate about passing on something they believe in. They are gifted communicators and great at making new contacts, often on the spur of the moment. They don't mind causing offense if it helps their cause. Evangelists seek out and love spending time with people who haven't heard the Good News. They know the Word and can make it relevant and accessible. They provoke and encourage other Christians in their witness and give them boldness.

They enjoy networking beyond the church, robust discussion, sharing their point of view and stimulating others to witness.

Words that describe them are sowing, persuading, enthusiastic, people-gathering. Reflect on times in your life when you have functioned as an evangelist:

_____

_____

_____

_____

_____

_____

_____

_____

_____

_____

_____

_____

_____

_____

_____

_____

_____

Some examples from the Bible:

Jesus—with the Samaritan woman and Nicodemus (John 3-4)

The servant-girl—she told Namaan, "I know a man who can heal you" (2 Kings 5)

The Samaritan woman—her testimony caused many in her community to come to Jesus (John 4:39-42)

Philip—the fast-moving Evangelist (Acts 8: 5, 26-40; 21:8)

Salespeople, enthusiastic story-tellers, journalists, stand-up comedians, marketing consultants—can you recognize evangelists among the people you know? What are some things these men and women have in common?

This may not be your natural role, but now that you've reflected on Biblical examples, can you think of times in your life when you've had to act in this way? How might you use this ministry gift in the future?

_____

_____

_____

_____

_____

_____

_____

_____

_____

_____

_____

_____

_____

Always be prepared to give an answer to everyone
who ask you to give the reason for the hope that you have.
1 Peter 3:15

According to this verse, what is every believer's responsibility related to evangelism?

_____

_____

_____

_____

_____

Going further …

And further …

The Pentagon: Pastor

✍

What is a pastor? Pastors are people who recognize the needs in other people and are able to comfort, challenge, and bring about change. They like to organize others to do these things, too. Pastors long to see Christians grow to their full potential. As shepherds, they have a rod as well as a staff and so confront areas that need to change. They can easily empathize with others and stimulate them to care.

They enjoy seeing others grow, one-on-one chats, showing hospitality, speaking the truth in love.

Words that describe them are caring, sensitive, loving, confronting, and supporting. Relate some times in your life when God has led you into the role of a pastor:

_____

_____

_____

_____

_____

_____

_____

_____

_____

_____

_____

_____

_____

_____

_____

_____

Some examples from the Bible:

Jesus—The good shepherd of the sheep (Matt. 9:36, John 10, 1 Pet. 5)

Jethro—father-in-law of Moses and management guru (Exod. 18)

Jonathan—friend and protector of David (1 Sam. 18-19)

Joanna, Susanna, and other women—support Jesus and his disciples out of their own means (Luke 8:1-3)

Barnabas—encourager extraordinaire (Acts 4:36, 15:36-39)

Counselors, social workers, nurses, life-coaches, foreign-aid workers—what are some things in common for these men and women? Can you recognize pastors among the people you know?

_____

_____

_____

_____

_____

_____

_____

_____

_____

_____

_____

_____

_____

_____

_____

_____

_____

_____

_____

This may not be your natural role, but now that you've reflected on Biblical examples, can you think of times in your life when you've had to act in this way? How might you use this ministry gift in the future?

_____

_____

_____

_____

_____

_____

_____

_____

_____

_____

_____

Read John 10 and compare the characteristics of the Good Shepherd to the role of a pastor:

_____

_____

_____

_____

_____

_____

_____

_____

_____

_____

_____

Going further …

And further …

THE PENTAGON: TEACHER

❧

What is a teacher? Teachers are people who encourage other people to go further, faster, higher, stronger than they have. They love to teach what they've learned and experienced and to see this impact other people's lives. They grasp truth, are excited by it and hold it out for others to receive. They provoke others to explore truth and invest in the next generation.

They enjoy reading and studying the Bible and helping others understand truth. They love to observe and learn from and about the things of life and pass this information on.

They inspire, train, coach, instruct, change, enlighten, and are considered wise. Describe some times in your life when you have functioned as a teacher:

_____

_____

_____

_____

_____

_____

_____

_____

_____

_____

_____

_____

_____

_____

_____

Some examples from the Bible:

Jesus—often identified by others as *rabbi* or teacher (John 1:38)
Lois and Eunice—Timothy's grandmother and mother (2 Tim. 1:5)
Apollos—fast learner and teacher (Acts 18:24-28)
Solomon—sage and king (1 Kings 10:23)
Ezra—trainer in the Law (Nehemiah 8)

Lecturers, trainers, coaches, demonstrators, teachers—what are some charaacteristics these men and women have in common? Who do you know that fits the description of a teacher?

_____

_____

_____

_____

_____

_____

_____

_____

_____

_____

_____

_____

_____

_____

_____

_____

_____

_____

_____

_____

_____

_____

_____

This may not be your natural role, but now that you've reflected on biblical examples, can you think of times in your life when you've had to act in this way? How might you use this ministry gift in the future?

_____

_____

_____

_____

_____

_____

_____

_____

_____

_____

_____

_____

"We are not all called to be teachers,
but we are all called to hold out the Truth."
A PASSIONATE LIFE, CHAPTER 16

What does it mean to "hold out the Truth" and how can you do that more effectively in your current life situations and relationships?

_____

_____

_____

_____

_____

_____

Going further …

And further …

THE HEXAGON:
INTRODUCTION

"Our Father in heaven, hallowed be your name,

your kingdom come, your will be done
on earth as it is in heaven.

Give us today our daily bread.

Forgive us our debts,
as we also have forgiven our debtors.

And lead us not into temptation,

but deliver us from the evil one."

MATTHEW 6:9-13

Have you noticed how six-sided shapes fit together perfectly? This pattern can be seen in a honeycomb where each three-dimensional hexagon fits with the next one and contains honey. Proverbs 24:13 says, "Eat honey, my son, for it is good; honey from the comb is sweet to your taste."

Honey is sweet to the taste—it has an immediate effect on the taste buds. Honey on the comb is chewy, allowing greater time for rumination. In the same way, The Lord's Prayer has both immediate and longer-term impact. As you study, enjoy, and go deeper with The Lord's Prayer, you will have your own stories to tell about the richness of praying the way Jesus taught us.

Forget your associations with The Lord's Prayer for a moment. What sweet things does Jesus tell us we can ask for from the Father? How can you begin to see his perpetual provision in your life in these six lines of prayer?

_____

_____

_____

_____

_____

_____

_____

_____

_____

_____

_____

Jesus taught his disciples to pray to his Father, just as Jesus prayed. It is about a relationship. The disciples asked Jesus to teach them how to pray because they clearly saw something different in Jesus' relationship with his Father. It is the perfect model for us to learn to relate to God (Up). How do you relate to God now? Is your relationship similar to the one described in this prayer?

_____

_____

_____

_____

_____

_____

_____

_____

_____

If your experience with The Lord's Prayer has been primarily reciting it from memory on a regular basis or on certain occasions, it may have become so familiar that it neither tastes sweet to you nor does it impact below the surface of your life. Tasteless and stale prayer is ineffectual if your goal is to live passionately for Jesus.

Think about times when prayer has lost its flavor for you—when it's grown stale. Have those times been matched by a similar staleness in your spiritual life? How have you worked through those "unsweetened" times?

When Jesus says, "Pray like this," we need to pay attention. As we look at The Lord's Prayer, phrase by phrase, our prayer is that your eyes will begin to brighten (1 Sam. 14:29). God's living word is meant to refresh and nourish us.

How sweet are your words to my taste,
sweeter than honey to my mouth!
PSALM 119:103

Going further ...

_____
_____
_____
_____
_____
_____
_____
_____
_____

And further ...

_____
_____
_____
_____
_____
_____
_____
_____

THE HEXAGON:
THE FATHER'S CHARACTER

"Our Father in heaven, hallowed be your name,

*your kingdom come, your will be done
on earth as it is in heaven.*

Give us today our daily bread.

*Forgive us our debts,
as we also have forgiven our debtors.*

And lead us not into temptation,

but deliver us from the evil one."

MATTHEW 6:9-13

Our. Isn't it amazing how much can be communicated in one small word? In that one word, Jesus tells us that, in prayer, we can converse with someone we have a personal relationship with—his Father, whose character we have yet to fully discover. Your Father, Jesus' Father, our Father. How does the fact that this prayer starts with the word "our" impact you?

_____

_____

_____

_____

_____

_____

_____

_____

_____

_____

Father—a name that contains so much meaning, so many images, so many memories. The word Jesus uses in this context is *Abba*, which literally means "daddy." Using this word in prayer would have shocked Jesus' listeners as it indicates an incredible closeness to God. "Our Father" could be expressed "Our daddy." It is a word that helps define the relationship God desires to have with us.

Jesus' relationship with his Father was so close that he called him "daddy." When you talk with God, are you able to think of him in affectionate terms? Why or why not?

_____

_____

_____

_____

_____

_____

_____

_____

Jesus taught us to pray to a real person in a real place—"Our Father in Heaven." Heaven is not limited to a "space up there." Heaven is God's home and reflects his character just as your home reflects who you are. It shows that, as close as God is to us, he is the I AM that is distinctly higher. How might this affect the way you present your prayers?

_____

_____

_____

_____

_____

If the opening phrase of The Lord's Prayer reveals the potential for intimacy with our Heavenly Father, God with us, the next phrase shows us that God is beyond our humdrum existence: ". . . hallowed be your name."

Moses experienced the hallowed nature of God when God spoke to him from the burning bush and again on Mount Sinai—an encounter which left Moses' countenance so altered that he had to wear a veil because the radiance of his face frightened the people (Exodus 34:29-35).

> *And we, who with unveiled faces all reflect the Lord's glory,*
> *are being transformed into his likeness with ever-increasing glory,*
> *which comes from the Lord, who is the Spirit.*
> 2 CORINTHIANS 3:18

An encounter with our Holy God will not leave us unchanged! When you pray, how do you expect to be changed by your time in the glory of God's presence?

_____

_____

_____

_____

_____

_____

In many cultures, parents name their children in full expectation of who that person will become. This was true in Jesus' time as well. Jesus invites us to honor God's name in respect of "who God is." What are the names you want to ascribe to God which express both your present knowledge and your future expectation?

_____

_____

_____

_____

Going further …

And further …

THE HEXAGON:
THE FATHER'S KINGDOM

"Our Father in heaven, hallowed be your name,

**your kingdom come, your will be done
on earth as it is in heaven.**

Give us today our daily bread.

*Forgive us our debts,
as we also have forgiven our debtors.*

And lead us not into temptation,

but deliver us from the evil one."

MATTHEW 6:9-13

In Mark 1:15, Jesus said, "The kingdom of God is near." The kingdom of God represents God's rule over all he has created. The power of his sovereignty—his right to rule—is available to us. In what ways did Jesus' life express the kingdom of God? How would you like to see the kingdom of God come here on earth and in your life?

_____

_____

_____

_____

_____

_____

_____

_____

_____

[Jesus said] *"But seek his kingdom, and these things will be given to you as well ... for your Father has been pleased to give you the kingdom."*
LUKE 12:31-32

How can you invite God's kingdom into your life? Into the lives of people around you? Into your church and your community? Into your country? How can you live in anticipation that God will give it to you?

_____

_____

_____

_____

_____

_____

_____

_____

It's often easier to pray "your kingdom come" than "your will be done." Why is that? Praying "your will be done" indicates a laying down of your own will and saying, "It's not about me and what I want." So there is an internal barrier of pride and self-reliance that is broken every time we pray and mean, "Your will be done."

Write down those areas where you need to pray, "Your will be done." Like Jacob (Genesis 32), you may need to wrestle with God in order to mean it wholeheartedly. An accountability partner can help you press through it.

_____

_____

_____

_____

_____

_____

The amazing reality is that after the struggle of praying, "Your will be done," we enter the realm of God's blessing for us. And we can pray, "Your will be done," in confidence because the Father wants what is best for us. So laying down our will is much better than continuing to go on in our own way.

Can you recognize times in your life when the dynamic of God's blessing in "Your will, not mine" has taken place? Write them down and give thanks.

_____

_____

_____

_____

_____

_____

_____

_____

_____

_____

_____

_____

_____

_____

_____

_____

"Your kingdom come" confronts and conquers an *external* barrier that is the kingdom of Satan.

"Your will be done" conquers an *internal* barrier of independence from God.

Now pray, "Your kingdom come, your will be done" into a situation which needs breakthrough.

Going further ...

And further ...

THE HEXAGON:
THE FATHER'S PROVISION

"Our Father in heaven, hallowed be your name,

*your kingdom come, your will be done
on earth as it is in heaven.*

Give us today our daily bread.

*Forgive us our debts,
as we also have forgiven our debtors.*

And lead us not into temptation,

but deliver us from the evil one."

MATTHEW 6:9-13

There is something about the smell of freshly baked bread wafting through the air that tantilizes our tastebuds, making us hungry. Warm kitchens, open fires, large tables and a sense of family—bread not only feeds our bodies, but when we share it with others, it feeds our souls. "Breaking bread" together often builds and strengthens the bonds of community.

Jesus shared bread with his followers and demonstrated the miraculous bounty of his Father by feeding the multitudes. When Jesus taught his disciples to pray, "Give us today our daily bread," he was instructing them to ask the Father for what they needed.

What do you need for today? Is it material provision? Is it time with your family? Is it that your work will satisfy? Is it that you will have enough to give away? Is it for a longing to be fulfilled?

_____

_____

_____

_____

_____

Now pray, "Give us today our daily bread," for someone you know:

_____

_____

_____

_____

_____

_____

Remember that your Father knows your needs before you ask for them (Matt. 6:8) but by asking, we proclaim that God is ultimately and in all ways our provider. Why is it gracious of God not to provide more than we need for each day? How do you daily acknowledge your dependence on him? How can you thank God for how he has met your needs today?

_____

_____

_____

_____

_____

_____

_____

_____

_____

_____

_____

_____

Then Jesus declared, "I am the bread of life. He who comes to me
will never go hungry, and he who believes in me will never be thirsty."
JOHN 6:35

This declaration follows Jesus' demonstration of compassion on the hunger of the multitudes. He was often moved by their physical needs but he never lost sight of his mission—to bring life. Jesus said, "I am the bread of life." Every time we pray this we're also praying Jesus' life into situations. What are you spiritually hungry for?

_____

_____

_____

_____

_____

_____

_____

_____

_____

_____

_____

_____

_____

_____

_____

_____

_____

_____

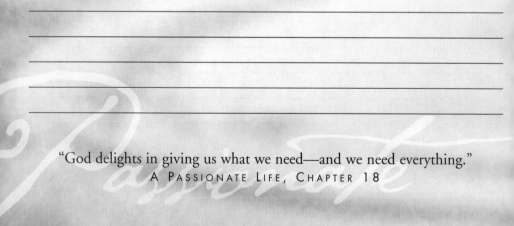

"God delights in giving us what we need—and we need everything."
A PASSIONATE LIFE, CHAPTER 18

Going further …

_____

_____

_____

_____

_____

_____

_____

_____

_____

_____

And further …

_____

_____

_____

_____

_____

_____

_____

_____

_____

_____

_____

THE HEXAGON:
THE FATHER'S FORGIVENESS

"Our Father in heaven, hallowed be your name,

*your kingdom come, your will be done
on earth as it is in heaven.*

Give us today our daily bread.

**Forgive us our debts,
as we also have forgiven our debtors.**

And lead us not into temptation,

but deliver us from the evil one."

MATTHEW 6:9-13

The Father expresses his forgiveness in the context of his eternal covenant with us—a relationship that he will never break. Nothing we can do is bad enough for him to stop wanting to be in relationship with us. We may be out of relationship with God, but he is never out of relationship with us.

Allow time for the reality of this to sink deep into your heart and then respond to his gift of relationship:

_____

_____

_____

_____

_____

_____

_____

_____

How does the following worship song, "I Will Offer Up My Life"
by Matt Redman, reflect your own feelings towards the covenant
relationship God offers you?

You deserve my every breath for You've paid the great cost;
Giving up Your life to death, even death on a cross.
You took all my shame away, there defeated my sin,
Opened up the gates of heav'n and have beckoned me in.

Jesus, what can I give, what can I bring
To so faithful a friend, to so loving a King?
Savior, what can be said, what can be sung
As a praise of Your name for the things You have done?
Oh my words could not tell, not even in part,
Of the debt of love that is owed by this thankful heart.

_____

_____

_____

_____

_____

_____

_____

_____

_____

_____

_____

_____

_____

_____

_____

_____

_____

It is in the light of the Father's forgiveness that we must extend forgiveness to those who have hurt or offended us. How often we react to hurt by pushing people immediately out of a relationship with us! However, this prayer presumes we have already forgiven "our debtors." There is an immediacy required of our forgiveness, as Paul writes in Ephesians 4:

> *Get rid of all bitterness, rage and anger, brawling and slander,*
> *along with every form of malice. Be kind and compassionate to one another,*
> *forgiving each other, just as in Christ God forgave you.*
> EPHESIANS 4:31-32

What is your first reaction when someone offends or hurts you? When has your first reaction had lasting consequences or results? How can changing your initial response speed the process of forgiveness towards others?

_____

_____

_____

_____

_____

_____

The word "debt" indicates a binding obligation. How is your obligation to forgive others connected to God's forgiveness? Read Matthew 18: 21-35.

_____

_____

_____

_____

_____

_____

_____

_____

Going further …

_____

_____

_____

_____

_____

_____

_____

_____

And further …

_____

_____

_____

_____

_____

_____

_____

_____

_____

_____

_____

THE HEXAGON:
THE FATHER'S GUIDANCE

"Our Father in heaven, hallowed be your name,

your kingdom come, your will be done
on earth as it is in heaven.

Give us today our daily bread.

Forgive us our debts,
as we also have forgiven our debtors.

And lead us not into temptation,

but deliver us from the evil one."

MATTHEW 6:9-13

Temptations are all around us, but as long as we don't engage with them, we are not falling into sin or running to danger. Jesus taught his disciples to pray for a way that leads away from temptation so that they would not fall back into the sins that had hindered them in the past.

Having another to whom we are accountable is a key way to keep from following after temptation. Once a temptation is brought "into the light," it is extremely difficult for the enemy to hold it over our heads or stir us up in a frenzy of guilt and shame.

What temptations are you currently facing in your life? Make a plan to talk these through with your accountability friend.

_____

_____

_____

_____

Your word is a lamp to my feet and a light for my path.
PSALM 119:105

According to the psalmist, God's Word is light to you in two specific ways—it both protects and guides. The beam of a flashlight illuminates the immediate rocks, stones and holes on the path at your feet which might hinder you or cause you to stumble. God shows you these things in detail so that you can avoid them and keep from falling.

What are the rocks and stones in your life which cause you to stumble? As the light of God's lamp at your feet reveals these stumbling blocks to you, bring them to him in prayer.

_____

_____

_____

_____

_____

_____

_____

_____

_____

_____

_____

_____

The word of God also shows you the big picture—it lights up the path ahead for the whole of your life—like the headlight on a car shows the direction you need to go.

The headlight reveals that God does have a plan and a way ahead—can you sense the excitement of this? Has God shown you more specifically what his path is for you?

As you spend time with God—reading Scripture, asking God for revelation by his Holy Spirit, talking with him in prayer—there is less room in your mind for unhealthy thought patterns which might trip you up or send you down wrong turns. Jesus said, "I am the light of the world," and "I am the way, the truth and the life." (John 8:12, 14:6) What have you discovered about God's guidance during your reflections?

Going further …

And further …

THE HEXAGON:
THE FATHER'S PROTECTION

"Our Father in heaven, hallowed be your name,

your kingdom come, your will be done
on earth as it is in heaven.

Give us today our daily bread.

Forgive us our debts,
as we also have forgiven our debtors.

And lead us not into temptation,

but deliver us from the evil one."

MATTHEW 6:9-13

This closing statement of The Lord's Prayer brings us to the frontline of battle again. We've recognized and invited God to make his kingdom evident here on earth, to push back the kingdom of darkness. Here Jesus asks his disciples to make an explicit request for the Father to deliver them from the evil one.

Jesus described the devil as the "prince of this world." In our world, we can see evidence of the destruction and suffering, sickness and death, which are clearly the domain of the evil one and have nothing to do with God's original plan.

How are the big sadnesses of our human lives—the loss of a loved one, the abuse of the innocent, the injustice to the poor, sickness and suffering for yourself or another—affecting you at the moment?

_____

_____

_____

_____

Jesus, a man of sorrows, showed that nothing that the enemy threw at him could prevail against the kingdom of God. He was tempted, lost his close friend Lazarus, had demons cry out against him, and his own people betray him. Yet, he won the great victory over the rule of Satan in our lives. He won for us eternal life where death has no more hold over us and there is no more crying.

"He will wipe every tear from their eyes. There will be no more death or mourning or crying or pain for the old order of things has passed away."
REVELATION 21:4

As you reflect on this verse, how does your view of the spiritual struggle change?

The eternal victory became a present reality. So when we pray, "Father, deliver us from the evil one," we pray in the confidence of Jesus' victory on the cross. It is finished and we won!

Which areas in your life need "Deliver us from the evil one" prayed over them? Pray this prayer for situations you know about in other people's lives and in your community and nation. Share these prayer needs with your accountability friend.

_____

_____

_____

_____

_____

_____

_____

_____

_____

_____

_____

_____

_____

_____

_____

_____

_____

_____

_____

For I am convinced that neither death nor life, nor angels nor demons, neither the present nor the future, nor any powers, neither height nor depth nor anything else in all creation, will be able to separate us from the love of God that is in Christ Jesus our Lord.

ROMANS 8:38-40

Going further …

Read 2 Corinthians 4: 7-10.

And further …

THE HEPTAGON:
MOVEMENT

*He who has the Son has life; he who does not have
the Son of God does not have life."*
1 JOHN 5:12

The Heptagon links the natural processes of biological life to spiritual
life. Just as Jesus often used examples from the natural world to illustrate
spiritual principles, we can use seven processes—Movement, Respiration,
Sensitivity, Growth, Reproduction, Excretion and Nutrition—as a spiritual
checklist for our spiritual vitality. You can use these seven processes as a
personal spiritual diagnostic and with your community to check how your
life together is developing.

What vital signs are currently evident in your life? Where are the signs
of life in your faith community?

God did this so that men would seek him and perhaps reach out
to him and find him, though he is not far from each one of us.
'For in him we live and move and have our being.'
Acts 17:27-28

Movement. Just as plants move towards light and water, so we need to move towards our source of light and life—God. Whenever we move physically, we exercise our muscles, including our heart. It's the same with spiritual movement. As individuals, we need to flex our spiritual muscles, especially our hearts, by moving in the three dimensions—our relationship with God (Up), our relationships within our faith community (In), and our relationship with others (Out).

We also need to come together to meet with him and to receive from him. In our communities of faith, it is vital that we actively move towards each other to deepen our relationships. Together with our communities, we need to move out into the world with God's love.

How are you actively moving towards the source of all light and life? What creative ideas can you introduce to refresh your worship as a community?

_____

_____

_____

_____

_____

_____

_____

_____

_____

_____

_____

_____

_____

_____

_____

_____

In your faith community, are you committed to the best for each other? Are you persistent in meeting together both socially as well as for worship? Why or why not?

_____

_____

_____

_____

_____

_____

_____

_____

As an individual, are your legs moving you beyond your comfort zone, and are your hands stretching out towards the poor? What are the areas you would like to reach out to?

_____

_____

_____

_____

_____

_____

_____

_____

_____

_____

_____

_____

_____

Going further …

And further …

THE HEPTAGON:
RESPIRATION

❧

Find a comfortable place to sit and take a few moments to relax. Ask God to take away any strains and stresses weighing on your mind at this moment. Make a conscious effort to release any burdens weighing on you. As you relax, become aware of your breathing and allow the natural rhythm of it to soothe you. Respiration—it's not something we normally sit around and take note of, yet it's essential to life.

What do you notice about your breathing?

_____

_____

_____

_____

_____

Now try different types of breathing: Take some long, deep breaths and notice the effect of that on your body. Now take several short, hurried breaths. What difference did you notice in your body's response?

_____

_____

_____

_____

Breathing is so natural, we normally don't even think about it but just try *not* breathing for a while! Go ahead, try holding your breath for as long as you can. Can you describe the reaction of your body?

_____

_____

_____

_____

We are rarely aware of our need to breathe during the normal course of daily living—it just occurs naturally because our bodies are programmed for it. In the same way, our relationship with the Holy Spirit often goes without our noticing but is essential to the whole of life. Often it's not until we are away from our regular routine that we take notice of the air we breathe.

"I've always been struck by the amazing clarity and sweetness of mountain air. As a city dweller, I love to take deep breaths of this air—breathing in a sense of purity and breathing out the stale remnants of city living. Breathing in the Holy Spirit is like having that mountain air available to you at all times."

—Liz

We can develop a normal pattern of deeply inhaling the Holy Spirit that can have the same effect on us spiritually as the refreshment of mountain air has on us physically. With discipline and practice, we can expand our capacity for spiritual respiration.

And with that [Jesus] *breathed on them and said,*
"Receive the Holy Spirit."
JOHN 20:22

How can you be more intentional about your respiration? How can you practice breathing in the Holy Spirit in new and deeper ways?

_____

_____

_____

_____

_____

_____

_____

_____

_____

Respiration consists not only of inhaling but of exhaling. It is the exchange of gases at the cell level within the body. It cleanses and renews cellular life essential to our bodies for movement. When you exhale, you make room in your lungs for fresh air to enter and clear out toxins. Respiration preserves and restores healthy life.

When you send your Spirit, they are created,
and you renew the face of the earth.
PSALM 104:30

What does spiritual exhaling look like for you? How does spiritual respiration affect your life together in your faith commuity?

_____

_____

_____

_____

_____

_____

_____

_____

_____

_____

_____

_____

_____

_____

_____

Breathe in deeply, receive the peace and power of the Holy Spirit from Jesus. Make part of your daily routine spending time in God's presence— as you become aware of his closeness, try to match your breathing to his.

Going further …

_____

_____

_____

_____

_____

_____

_____

_____

_____

_____

And further …

_____

_____

_____

_____

_____

_____

_____

_____

_____

_____

THE HEPTAGON:
SENSITIVITY

The sensitivity of our five senses trigger response signals. They give wholeness to life. All the senses can act to protect us, but there's more to it than that—they give us fullness of joy. For example, touch will save us from burning our hands, but touch also enriches our lives with wonderful sensations like the feeling of sand between our toes at the beach, the warm embrace of a loved one, or a refreshing splash of cool water on a hot day.

How does sensitivity apply in our spiritual checklist? Sensitivity is a daily gift to us from our Creator. It is our growing sensitivity to him that feeds our life and gives us joy.

You have made known to me the path of life;
you will fill me with joy in your presence,
with eternal pleasures at your right hand.
PSALM 16:11

Go through each of the five physical senses (touch, taste, sight, hearing, and smell) and write down the aspects you really enjoy about them.

_____

_____

_____

_____

_____

_____

_____

_____

_____

_____

Our physical senses heighten our awareness to the people and things that surround us. Sensitivity increases our perception and responsiveness in the three dimensions of our relationships—Up, In and Out. Here again we can look to Jesus as our example.

Read John 17:1-5. Jesus' relationship with his Father shows his sensitivity to what God asked him to do. In this prayer, what evidence do you see of Jesus' responsiveness to his Father?

_____

_____

_____

_____

_____

_____

_____

What is the Father asking you to do? Do you have a sense of satisfaction in completing the work the Father has entrusted to you?

_____

_____

_____

_____

_____

_____

_____

_____

_____

_____

_____

Read Mark 14:3-11. Jesus knew the reason why the woman had broken through all conventional behavior to express this loving action. He shows tenderness, another sign of sensitivity, in two ways:

1. to the woman—he knew why she was doing it and affirmed her.
2. to those present—he knew what they were thinking and challenged them.

Note the reaction of Judas Iscariot. Showing spiritual sensitivity makes us suseptible to misunderstanding. How do you react to Jesus' sensitivity? When have you demonstrated spiritual sensitivity to others only to be misunderstood?

_____

_____

_____

_____

_____

_____

_____

_____

Read Luke 19:41-48. These verses show different aspects of Jesus' sensitivity to the world of the lost, and how he responded to it.

What are the things that make you weep—where is your righteous anger? Are you moved to tears by the thought of people missing out on God's love? What are you going to do about it?

_____

_____

_____

_____

_____

_____

_____

Going further …

And further …

THE HEPTAGON:
GROWTH

*So then, just as you received Christ Jesus as Lord, continue to live in him,
rooted and built up in him, strengthened in the faith as you were taught,
and overflowing with thankfulness.*
COLOSSIANS 2:6

If you look at a plant you can see two types of growth—there is the evident
change in size and shape as it grows bigger, sprouts leaves, and bears
fruit—and there is the unseen growth of the roots reflecting the plant's
general maturity and health. A plant may sprout up very quickly but unless
it also growths healthy and deep roots, it will die.

In our spiritual lives, there are moments when we recognize quick visible
growth and other times when we know that God deepens our roots. In which
stage are you at the moment?

_____
_____
_____
_____
_____
_____
_____
_____
_____
_____
_____
_____
_____

Growth happens throughout our lives. Physically, it happens most obviously during our childhood and teenage years. Growth spurts are often associated with an increased appetite. Sudden growth can leave us feeling uncomfortable and gangly. None of our clothes fit, and we have to put up with relatives and friends saying, "My, haven't you grown!?" We need to learn how to live comfortably in our new size.

Likewise, in our spiritual journey, we have sudden spurts of spiritual growth, which may leave us feeling uncomfortable. It's important that we learn to live in this new dimension by allowing God to mature us. Both of these processes — growth spurts and times of maturing — continue throughout our lives if we choose to engage with God's plan.

Do you recognize this pattern of growth and maturing in your own life? How do you handle the awkwardness and discomfort associated with growth?

_____

_____

_____

_____

_____

_____

As you look at your community of faith, when have you experienced times of rapid and visible growth, adding new people to your numbers? How did you handle the discomfort of accommodating these extra people?

_____

_____

_____

_____

_____

_____

_____

"My favorite tree is the beech. In the winter, I can see its strong, sturdy trunk reaching upwards and outwards to the sky—a beautiful silhouette on a winter's evening. I'm aware that from its base there are roots that go deep down into the soil below. In the spring, the particular shade of green as the buds open up speaks to me of a lavish Creator. There is a season of vigorous growth into the summer when the leaves become darker and deeper, giving shelter and protection to the birds and animals who live in the canopy. In the fall, the golden brown leaves and the falling beech nuts remind me of creativity and fruitfulness even in a season of dying. I often pray that God will make me like a beech tree—that my roots will dig deep down into his Word for nourishment, that my trunk and my branches will reach up towards my Creator God, and that I will live in seasons of vigorous growth and fruitfulness."

—Liz

What spiritual season are you in? What is God calling you to do during this season?

_____

_____

_____

_____

_____

_____

_____

_____

_____

_____

_____

_____

_____

_____

_____

_____

_____

Going further …

And further …

THE HEPTAGON:
REPRODUCTION

cĝ

"For God so loved the world that he gave his one and only Son,
that whoever believes in him shall not perish but have eternal life."
JOHN 3:16

The essence of reproduction is the multiplication of life. God created this process out of his love for us. It is part of his blessing on man at creation and, in God's perfect plan, occurs in the context of loving relationships. Reproduction, according to God's plan, forms an unbreakable bond—one of love, responsibility, and self-sacrifice.

What are some of the joys and blessings you have experienced related to the reproduction of life, either physical (as in parenting) or spiritual (as in discipleship)? Take time to thank God for the life he has given you in Jesus:

_____

_____

_____

_____

_____

_____

_____

_____

_____

_____

_____

_____

_____

_____

_____

The basis of reproduction is to recreate or pass on the life that God gives you. We see this in examples throughout the Bible: Moses to Joshua, Elijah to Elisha, and Priscilla and Aquila to Apollos, Lydia to her household, Philip to the Ethiopian eunuch.

We clearly see one generation investing in the next in the life of Timothy. When he was a child, Timothy's mother, Eunice, and his grandmother, Lois, passed their faith on to him and nurtured him in it (2 Tim. 1: 3-5).

Jesus multiplied life in his disciples by pouring himself into them. He left the active memory of bread and wine, which continues to bring life to us today. Paul introduces his account of the Last Supper with the words:

For I received from the Lord what I also passed on to you ...
1 CORINTHIANS 11:23

Who has reproduced the life he or she has in God by passing it on to you? How did he or she do it?

_____

_____

_____

_____

_____

_____

_____

_____

_____

_____

_____

_____

_____

_____

Then Paul, recognizing Timothy's faith, discipled him in all he knew, continuing this process of reproduction (1 and 2 Timothy).

To whom do you want to pass your faith? How are you actively working to reproduce your faith in others' lives? How seriously does your faith community take spiritual reproduction in the context of loving relationships?

_____

_____

_____

_____

_____

_____

_____

_____

_____

Look back at the square. The square shows us the way Jesus invested in his disciples. When we are reproducing ourselves in whatever context, the square is the key tool for passing on what we have learned.

Spend time asking God if there are people in your community of faith who you could disciple. Begin by praying for them:

_____

_____

_____

_____

_____

_____

_____

_____

Going further …

And further …

THE HEPTAGON:
EXCRETION

❧

Surely you desire truth in the inner parts;
you teach me wisdom in the inmost place.
PSALM 51:6

Excretion rids waste products from our bodies that would otherwise harm us. When we sweat, for example, the pores of our skin release toxins that if left trapped inside would eventually kill us. The topic of excretion is a sensitive subject. We don't like to think about waste products building up inside our bodies. In much the same way, we don't like to admit that we lust, lie, idolize or hurt the heart of God with our sinful nature. Simply ignoring these things, however, won't make them go away.

Think of excretion as playing a vital role in our spiritual health. When we store up feelings of anger, bitterness and unforgiveness, we close our spiritual pores, allowing sin to pollute our lives in Christ.

Read 1 Peter 2:1 and Galatians 5:19-21. Concentrate on how each of these spiritual toxins affects your life. Take it a step further. Think how they affect the lives of others, perhaps those you love the most. Be truthful as you fill in your response below.

_____

_____

_____

_____

_____

_____

_____

_____

_____

_____

Take a moment to think about the things we do regularly to keep healthy and free of toxins. Regular dental visits help prevent tooth decay as well as gum disease. The hygienist carefully scrapes and flosses around each tooth, loosening and cleansing away weeks of plaque and food build-up. Mmm, good! We leave the experience feeling clean and refreshed.

Similarly, "sin build-up" must be removed from our bodies. If it is not, it will weaken our spritiual health. We need God to take us through the process of repentance and forgiveness to keep us healthy and energized to do his will.

Describe a time when anger, envy or holding a grudge sapped your strength and energy making it virtually impossible to love and serve others. As you do, contemplate on how "sin build-up" is contrary to the peace and joy that Christ offers all who believe in him.

*...let us draw near to God with a sincere heart in full assurance
of faith having our hearts sprinkled to cleanse us from a guilty conscience
and having our bodies washed with pure water.*
HEBREWS 10:22

Do you believe that "sin build-up" is a necessary way of life for you? Reflect on a time when the Lord cleansed you of bitterness and ill will. What did that experience feel like?

_____

_____

_____

_____

_____

_____

_____

_____

_____

_____

_____

_____

_____

_____

_____

_____

_____

_____

We cannot rid ourselves of sin no matter how hard we try. Spiritual cleansing is the work of the Holy Spirit–and we need him to do it. Through faith, repentance and prayer we go to the throne room of our Heavenly Father who promises to wash us clean with pure, living water.

Going further …

_____

_____

_____

_____

_____

_____

_____

_____

_____

_____

And further …

_____

_____

_____

_____

_____

_____

_____

_____

_____

_____

THE HEPTAGON:
NUTRITION

❧

*After all, no one ever hated his own body, but he feeds
and cares for it, just as Christ does the church.*
EPHESIANS 5:29

Nutrition isn't simply about food—it's about feeding the body with things
that are good for it. In a fast food culture, it's easy to eat to pander to an
appetite without satisfying. Eating the wrong types of food and eating irregu-
larly makes us sluggish, irritable, hyper, irregular in our excretion, and either
stunts our growth or causes a "supersize" me.

Healthy eating is about looking after the bodies that God has created.
We need a balanced, healthy diet both spiritually and physically. Healthy
eating is tasty to the body and the spirit. It's not about feeding your own
needs—it's allowing God to feed you.

What do you notice about the way you feel when you are eating healthily?
How does your energy level change when you eat poorly? Why might your
eating habits be important to your spiritual health?

_____

_____

_____

_____

_____

_____

_____

_____

_____

_____

_____

_____

Meanwhile his disciples urged him, "Rabbi, eat something."
But he said to them, "I have food to eat that you know nothing about."
Then his disciples said to each other, "Could someone have brought him food?"
"My food," said Jesus, "is to do the will of him who sent me
and to finish his work."
JOHN 4:31-34

What about spiritual food—do you have a healthy, balanced diet?
What nourishes you spiritually?

_____

_____

_____

_____

_____

_____

Community is an important part of nutrition. A lot of Jesus' life was spent
eating with friends. How often do you share a meal with someone? How often
do you eat alone? Does your family prefer good conversation during meals or
TV trays and the evening news? Do you open your home to others?

_____

_____

_____

_____

_____

_____

_____

_____

_____

_____

"Then the King will say to those on his right, 'Come, you who are blessed by my Father; take your inheritance, the kingdom prepared for you since the creation of the world. For I was hungry and you gave me something to eat, I was thirsty and you gave me something to drink, I was a stranger and you invited me in...'"
MATTHEW 25:34-35

Read Galatians 5:22-23. Ask God to feed you with these fruits.

MRS GREN

These seven life processes are interconnected. They work together and affect each other. They do not work in isolation. You can't have growth or movement or excretion or reproduction or sensitivity or respiration without effective nutrition.

Take each one of the processes in turn, and consider how it affects and is affected by the other six. Think in both spiritual and physical terms:

Going further …

And further …

THE OCTAGON:
PERSON OF PEACE

W here the Hexagon gives us a deeper insight into our relationship with God (Up) and the Heptagon into our relationships with our friends (In), the Octagon unpacks the Out dimension. Jesus instructed his disciples to go out in pairs, and to look for the Person of Peace (Luke 9-10). As we go out into our world, we can do no better than follow this strategy—going out with our community perceiving the People of Peace God gives to us.

How do you recognize People of Peace? They are the people who welcome you, show you hospitality, and indicate they want to be with you. They may not make you feel peaceful and may not be peaceful people in themselves, but they are people who are clearly open to you and moving towards you.

"There are several People of Peace at our local supermarket where I do my weekly shopping. I'm a naturally chatty person, so I end up talking to the checkout assistants. One in particular seemed to enjoy our conversation, so the following week I went back to her. Over the years she has gotten to know when I am having parties, whether I am entertaining young people or older people and the birthdays/celebrations in our family. She tells me when there are special offers I have missed and asks me about new foods which I might be trying out."

—Liz

Read Luke 10:1-24. What do these verses tell you about a Person of Peace?

_____

_____

_____

_____

_____

It's important to ask God to develop our skills of perception as we look for People of Peace. Perceiving the advances and withdrawals of people around us allows us to easily recognize open and closed doors of opportunity. For example, someone in your office may offer to get you a cup of coffee or a neighbor may pause to chat at the mailbox—a simple act which can be an early indication that this individual is a Person of Peace.

It's so easy in the busyness of life to miss these simple signs. That's why we need God to illuminate these occurrences so that we don't miss them. Reflect on recent encounters you have had with nonbelievers and check for signs of a Person of Peace:

_____

_____

_____

_____

_____

_____

_____

_____

_____

_____

_____

_____

_____

_____

_____

_____

_____

_____

"I used to think that Jesus' command, "Go and make disciples," meant that I had to go to the most testing people I could think of. I viewed it all as a challenge. When I first heard about "People of Peace," it opened up a whole new area of possibilities to me. If I simply perceived what was going on around me, I could start to spot People of Peace and allow God to develop relevant relationships, which naturally lead to conversations about faith."

—Anne

Ask God to increase your skills of perception. Are there additional People of Peace you now recognize?

_____

_____

_____

_____

_____

_____

_____

Remember, it is God's responsibility to prepare the heart of the Person of Peace. How does knowing that empower you to actively seek the Person of Peace? How can you know what message God has for you to give to the Person of Peace?

_____

_____

_____

_____

_____

_____

"'Lord, bring into my path today a Person of Peace, and give me the grace and courage to speak your words to this person.'"

Going further …

And further …

THE OCTAGON:
PASSING AND PERMANENT

❧

Jesus met many people along his life-path.. He recognized when someone was open to him, and he immediately reached out to him or her. These were "passing" relationships—people like the woman at the well, Zacchaeus, the woman with the issue of blood, the rich young ruler, various blind men, assorted lepers, the boy with the loaves and fishes and we could go on and on.

Jesus also had permanent relationships with people who stayed with him for the long haul—people like Mary, Martha and Lazarus, the disciples, his mother, his brothers, the women who provided for him (Luke 8).

Some examples of Passing Relationships:

"A few years ago, soon after my father had died, I went to a picture framing shop to have a painting, which reminded me of my dad, framed. The lady in the shop recognized the place in the painting and I told her about my father. She then told me about her mother who had died a couple of days before my father. In that moment, we shared something deep together, and I told her I would pray for her."

—Liz

"During 'Mission Week' at our church, we were going out in twos around the city asking God for opportunities to pray for people. As Martin and I walked along a street, we witnessed a man being beaten up by thugs. He managed to escape from them and ran towards us and collapsed at out feet. We didn't have to look much further for an opportunity to bring good news into somebody's life! We took him to the hospital, chatted with him while we were waiting and explained why we had been there at that time. He then talked about other times in his life when he knew that God had intervened, and he invited us to meet the rest of his family."

—Anne

Some examples of Permanent Relationships:

"I worked in the same office with Susan for three years. During that time, she started to notice that my lifestyle was different. For example, one day I offered to do a hotel booking for another colleague, Mark, who was amazed that I would take time out of my busy schedule to help him. When I left the office, Susan explained to Mark, "Anne's done that because she's a Christian and that's the type of thing that Christians do." They (and the rest of the office) then had a twenty-minute conversation about the impact of Christianity on someone's life. During the rest of the time Susan and I worked together, we started to have more and more conversations about faith. A year after I left the company, I received a letter from her saying she had joined an "Alpha" group at her local church and that she had come to believe in Jesus! Thanks be to God!"

—Anne

"For several years I have been going to the same beautician, Rebecca. She did my wedding make-up, and I have been a loyal customer since then. She's a very 'spiritual' person, and in between our conversations about children, holidays, clothes, and work, she showed interest in my spiritual life. I don't feel I have to hide anything from her about my relationship with Jesus, and in fact, she even knows that I consider her a Person of Peace."

—Liz

Describe some "passing" relationships in your life:

_____

_____

_____

_____

_____

_____

_____

_____

Describe some "permanent" relationships in your life:

_____

_____

_____

_____

_____

_____

You may have noticed in our examples from Jesus' relationships that we included some who did not respond to his message during his lifetime. The rich young ruler was a passing acquaintance and he turned away from Jesus' call. (Matt. 19:16-22)

Jesus had permanent relationships with his brothers, yet they did not believe him while he was alive. John 7:3-5

It's freeing to know that not everyone accepted Jesus' words and actions.

_____

_____

_____

_____

_____

_____

Although you may "sow the seed" in either passing or permanent relationships, you may not necessarily be the one who "reaps the harvest."

I planted the seed, Apollos watered it, but God made it grow.
1 CORINTHIANS 3:6

Keep on scattering seeds liberally and allow God to be the Lord of the harvest. (Luke 8:4-15)

Going further …

And further …

THE OCTAGON:
PROCLAMATION AND PRESENCE

❧

[Jesus said,] *"The Spirit of the Lord is on me, because he has anointed me to preach good news to the poor. He has sent me to proclaim freedom for the prisoners and recovery of sight for the blind, to release the oppressed, to proclaim the year of the Lord's favor."*
LUKE 4:18-19

He brought good news of the kingdom of God into people's lives by the words he spoke and by his actions—the way he lived his life.

When we find our People of Peace, we have opportunities to speak God's word (proclamation) and to be God's truth in their lives (presence). In passing relationships, it is mostly (but not always) proclamation that occurs; in permanent relationships, it is mainly (but again not always) presence that brings change.

What do these two words "proclaim" and "presence" mean to you?

_____

_____

_____

_____

_____

We all have likely experienced new Christians who, in their enthusiasm to share Jesus, spend a lot of time telling their families (i.e. their permanent relationships) what they should believe. This often leads to resentment on the part of the family members and understandably so. What they wanted to see is evidence of a changed life. We heard a Muslim woman recently say that when her son became a Christian, he kept phoning her saying she needed to get to know Jesus. But it wasn't until she visited him and saw the difference in his life that she wanted to get to know Jesus for herself.

Think about times when your presence has made a difference.

_____

_____

_____

_____

_____

"A mentor at work once said to me, 'I don't know whether you realize this, Anne, but you bring peace when you walk into a room. I've seen two directors having an argument, and when you walk in, the argument stops and peace is there.' The peace that Jesus gives me has always been important to me, and I guess that's what this mentor saw—a gift that God had given me."

—Anne

There are also times when it's clear that you need to declare God's Word and verbally share how Jesus has changed your life. It's also a time to question a person about whether he or she wants to get to know God. Words from God bring truth—it may be a scripture, it may be a word of revelation like prophecy or an offer to pray for healing then and there. It may even be a word of challenge. We have a friend who has the ability to ask direct, open questions that make people think about God—What do you think about God? Have you ever prayed? Do you think this is all there is to life? Conversations develop from there, giving opportunities to say, "God is near to you."

Think about times where you have been able to proclaim God's word.

_____

_____

_____

_____

_____

_____

_____

"I went to do some clothes shopping and started chatting with the assistant. She told me about some recent events in her life that had caused her a lot of pain. I felt God urging me to tell her about Jesus. I was not to talk about church or what I did on Sunday—I had to say the name of Jesus to her, and I had to be direct. I said, "I think you need Jesus!" She said, "I think you're right." And I prayed for her then and there."

—Liz

In both "proclamation" and "presence," we have to rely on God to give us the confidence and grace to express his love in either words or actions or both. It would be a mistake to think that these things are easy—we need to ask for boldness and courage. Why don't you do that now?

_____

_____

_____

_____

_____

_____

_____

_____

_____

_____

_____

_____

_____

_____

_____

_____

_____

Read the story of Ananias and Paul in Acts 9:1-19. Praise God for Ananias' obedience!

Going further …

And further …

THE OCTAGON:
POWER AND PREPARATION

Sometimes God uses his power in a startling way to bring people to himself. The story of Saul's conversion is an obvious example. (Acts 9:1-6)

There are other times when God prepares a person for years before he or she has faith. James, one of Jesus' brothers, is an example of that. Jesus' life prepared him, but he came to faith after Jesus' death and grew to be one of the leaders of the early church.

God can use us in both startling and preparatory ways to work in people's lives.

Power

God's power is made evident through healing, prophetic revelation, dreams and visions and major *kairos* events like the birth of a child, moving home or a sudden crisis—anything that causes us to turn to God and say, "That is amazing!" (Mark 1:27) or "Help! I need your power!" (Luke 18:38).

Write down events where God's power has been evident to you.

_____

_____

_____

_____

_____

_____

_____

[Jesus said to his disciples,] *"But you will receive power when the Holy Spirit comes on you; and you will be my witnesses in Jerusalem, and in all Judea and Samaria, and to the ends of the earth."*

ACTS 1:8

Pray for God's power to be evident in your life and in your relationships.

_____

_____

_____

_____

"I visited the hairdresser recently and one of the assistants was complaining that her wrist was extremely sore. I prayed silently to God, "If you want me to pray for healing for her, please, can you clear the other people out of this part of the room." Never give God a challenge! The room cleared very quickly, leaving Amanda and me alone. I said to her, "Would you like me to pray for you wrist now?" She said, "Yes," and I placed my hand on her wrist and asked Jesus to heal the pain. As I did that, her wrist became hot. She exclaimed, "What's that!?" I replied, "That's the Holy Spirit at work healing your wrist." When the others came back in she told them all about this and by the end of my appointment her wrist was better. Praise God!"

—Anne

Preparation

Preparing soil for planting takes a long time and a lot of energy. Many people may turn over the soil of a person's heart before a seed is able to take root and grow. Each action on our part is like one turn of the soil. These actions can include: inviting people to barbeques, playing different sports, setting up a fair trade event, having series on parenting or ethics in the workplace (using Christian principles), having an Alpha course, going to the movies/theatre together....

Think about Nicodemus for a moment. He was often present when Jesus taught and healed. This turned the soil of his heart so that eventually, late at night, he went to see Jesus. (John 3:1-21)

How did God prepare you to receive his word?

_____

_____

_____

_____

Ask for inspiration for different ways of "turning the soil" in the lives of your People of Peace.

_____

_____

_____

_____

_____

_____

"Going out for an informal meal with business associates can be a turn of the soil. John and I have had many such pleasurable meals with business friends. Although we may not have seen seeds grow, we have seen soil turn in people's lives including our own."

—Liz

Read Luke 1:26–56.

Consider God's preparation in Mary's life so that when his power "overshadowed" her, she responded obediently and joyfully.

Are we allowing God to prepare our hearts so that we receive his power? Are we praying that for our community of faith, our People of Peace, and for all those who don't yet know Jesus?

_____

_____

_____

To summarize, the Octagon shows how we perceive who our People of Peace are, how we interact with them through the nature of our relationships (passing/permanent), ways we bring good news (proclamation/presence), and God's inspiration(power/preparation).

Going further …

And further …

A PASSIONATE LIFE

❧

*"I have come that they may have life, and have it to the full. I am
the good shepherd. The good shepeherd lays down his life for the sheep."*
JOHN 10:10-11

LifeShapes helps us learn, remember, and teach the discipleship principles
that Jesus taught and lived. By following them—from the Circle to the
Square to the Octogon—we are better equipped to live the life God intends
for us, a life of abundance and passion. The passionate life is one of surrender—laying down our selves and taking up the cross of Jesus daily.

What areas of your life do you need to surrender to God? What does
"taking up the cross of Jesus" mean to you?

_____

_____

_____

_____

_____

_____

_____

_____

_____

_____

_____

_____

_____

_____

_____

"A passionate walk with Jesus."
What have you learned about walking with Jesus?

_____

_____

_____

_____

_____

_____

"A passionate faith that spills over into everything we do."
How have you seen you faith start to spill over into the everyday areas
of your life?

_____

_____

_____

_____

_____

_____

"A passionate energy for the kingdom of God."
What evidence of new or renewed energy for the kingdom have you seen?

_____

_____

_____

_____

_____

_____

"A passionate conviction to minister to those around you."

What new convictions have developed about ministering to others around you?

_____

_____

_____

_____

_____

_____

_____

_____

_____

_____

"A passionate search for others ready to meet Jesus."

What have you discovered about God's desire towards the lost and how you can participate in his search for them?

_____

_____

_____

_____

_____

_____

_____

_____

_____

_____

"A passionate life."

Going further …

And further …

Additional copies of this and other Honor products
are available wherever good books are sold.

Other titles in this series:
God's Answer to Your Deepest Longings
God's Invitation to a Meaningful Life

If you have enjoyed this book,
or if it has had an impact on your life,
we would like to hear from you.

Please contact us at:
Honor Books
Cook Communications Ministries, Dept. 201
4050 Lee Vance View
Colorado Springs, CO 80918

Or visit our Web site:
www.cookministries.com

HONOR **HB** BOOKS
Inspiration and Motivation for the Seasons of Life